Ceramics for Kids

Ceramics for Kids

Creative Clay Projects to Pinch, Roll, Coil, Slam & Twist

Mary Ellis

LARK BOOKS

A Division of Sterling Publishing Co., Inc.

New York

Editor:
Suzanne J. E. Tourtillott

Art Direction & Production:
Tom Metcalf

Production Assistant:
Shannon Yokely

Photography:
Evan Bracken

Cover Design:
Barbara Zaretsky

Assistant Editors:
Veronika Alice Gunter
Rain Newcomb
Heather Smith

10 9 8 7 6 5 4 3 2 1
First Edition
CIP Available

Published by Lark Books, a division of
Sterling Publishing Co., Inc.
387 Park Avenue South, New York, N.Y. 10016

© 2002, Mary Ellis

Distributed in Canada by Sterling Publishing, c/o Canadian Manda Group, One Atlantic Ave.,
Suite 105 Toronto, Ontario, Canada M6K 3E7

Distributed in the U.K. by Guild of Master Craftsman Publications Ltd., Castle Place, 166 High Street,
Lewes, East Sussex, England BN7 1XU
Tel: (+ 44) 1273 477374, Fax: (+ 44) 1273 478606, Email: pubs@thegmcgroup.com, Web:
www.gmcpublications.com

Distributed in Australia by Capricorn Link (Australia) Pty Ltd., P.O. Box 704, Windsor,
NSW 2756, Australia

If you have questions or comments about this book, please contact:
Lark Books
67 Broadway
Asheville, NC 28801
(828) 236-9730

Printed in Hong Kong

ISBN 1-57990-198-0

Contents

Introduction

Have you ever held a piece of cool, soft clay in your hand? It's so easy to start working it with your fingers to make a face, a bird, or a bowl. In fact, for thousands of years, people have been doing just that. Go to a museum, and you will probably see pottery from all over the world that dates back many thousands of years.

Today, people have electric kilns and wheels and other equipment to help them make pottery. But the basics haven't changed. We still use our hands, and we still use clay from the earth to make more objects than you can imagine—some useful, some beautiful, some weird. After you've seen some pottery in a museum, try going to an art or craft gallery to see what modern-day potters are making. You'll probably be surprised by all the differ-

ent shapes and colors and textures that are possible with clay.

For that matter, you don't have to go to a museum or gallery to see the great variety of clay objects. Look around your house. From the flowerpots to the bathroom tiles, clay is everywhere. Did you know that even the space shuttle Discovery is protected by special tiles made from…you guessed it…clay!

Clay is here to stay. So let's see what we can do with this amazing material. The projects in this book will get you started. Try out a few, and you'll probably come up with plenty of your own ideas. Whether you're making these projects, or creating some of your own, don't be afraid to experiment. The great thing about clay is, if you don't like how something looks, you can always squish it up and try again!

This book will show you how to set up your own studio, how to make lots of different clay projects, and how to glaze and decorate them. Once your projects are glazed and fired, they will be hard and permanent like the pottery you see in museums and shops. Who knows? Maybe one of your creations will still be around thousands of years from now!

To Parents and Teachers...

It's hard to find a more inviting medium than clay. Clay is soft and cool to the touch, and easily sculpted and manipulated into many three-dimensional forms. Once clay is fired, it's hard, durable, and safe to eat or drink from. Making useful and beautiful ceramic pieces can give children a real feeling of satisfaction and accomplishment.

This book will show you and the child how to set up a pottery studio at home. He or she will learn how to handbuild with clay, how to make a variety of engaging projects, how to decorate with glazes and underglazes, and how to make and use a sawdust kiln.

Each project, designed for the beginner, contains detailed, step-by-step instructions. Don't think, though, that there's only one way to make the projects in this book. Once children get an understanding of what works—and doesn't work—with clay, they'll come up with their own ideas and solutions. The challenge, of course, is to provide just the right amount of help. Try making some of the projects yourself, so that you and the child work and learn side by side. Working with clay can be a relaxing social activity, as well as a chance for creative expression.

On a more practical note, clay crafts aren't especially expensive. Look through the materials list, and you'll see that most of the items needed can be found around the house. It's not necessary to buy a kiln (although I'll show you how to make a sawdust kiln from a metal trash can). Firing charges at a commercial pottery usually depend on how much space is used in the kiln. The charges are generally reasonable, even for large projects.

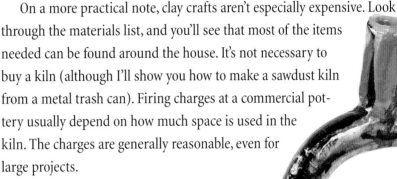

If you can't find a place to fire your child's projects, you might consider purchasing some self-hardening clay from a hobby shop. When it's moist, use self-hardening clay just like regular clay. After it dries and hardens, decorate it with acrylic paints. It will be reasonably hard, but not completely waterproof or safe to eat from. Self-hardening clay is more expensive than regular clay, so you might want to use it only for small projects.

Whether you're a parent or a teacher (or both), I hope you and your budding artist will find this book helpful, and that you'll enjoy exploring the many possibilities clay has to offer.

Getting Started

So you want to be a potter? No, not Harry Potter! A potter is an artist or craftsperson who makes clay pots, right? True, but potters don't just make flowerpots and stop there. By "pots," a potter might mean mugs, bowls, plates, casserole dishes, teapots, coffeepots, platters, boxes, goblets—even bathroom sinks! You can even make a dragon out of clay, or an animal-headed Egyptian ceremonial jar. If it's a useful clay object, it's called *functional*; if it's just neat to look at, it's called *decorative*. Flip through the pages of this book, and you'll see some unusual and fun projects. Before you dive in, though, it's a good idea to understand everything you can about clay. Let's start with the basics.

Where Does Clay Come From?

Clay comes from the earth, but it hides under the soil we usually see. All over the surface of our planet is a layer of dirt called topsoil. Topsoil has a lot of rotted leaves and other decayed plant matter in it and usually feels kind of grainy, like sand.

If you walk along an old dirt road, you might see a place where all the topsoil has been scraped away and underneath is some soft, sticky-feeling clay. What you're actually seeing is decomposed rock. Over thousands or perhaps millions of years, the rock mixed with water and eventually softened into clay. Depending on just what kind of rocks are under the topsoil where you live, the clay might be colored white, or bluish-gray, or even orange. If you pinch off some of the clay, it will bend and stretch without breaking.

You could actually create a pot or figure with some of the clay you found, but that would mean an awful lot of digging! And then you'd need to strain out all the sticks and hard chunks of rocks. Today, instead of spending all their time digging and cleaning, most potters buy their clay in big, plastic bags from a ceramic supply shop. The ingredients in this clay are the same as those of the clay you'd find under the topsoil, but it's been cleaned, so you can use it right away.

When potters heat the clay, they call it *firing*. Clay must get very hot before it gets hard. The oven in your kitchen won't get the clay nearly hot enough. Back before your grandparents were born, people used wood for fuel and burned, or fired, the pots for a long time to get them hot enough. Not only did they have to dig and clean the clay, they had to chop a lot of wood, too! Most potters today use special clay ovens called kilns that run on electricity or gas, and get much hotter than a regular cooking oven.

The Ceramic Process

As you might have guessed by now, there's a specific step-by-step process for making things from clay. When the clay is moist and soft, you can make it into many different shapes and change it however you want. If you get tired of working on it, you can always wrap it tightly in plastic and it will stay moist until you want to work on it again.

Once the clay dries out, though, you can't change the shape of it any more. The drier it gets, the more brittle it becomes, and you must be careful not to break it. You can tell how dry the clay is by how it feels and how it looks. As clay dries, it gets lighter in color, and it feels harder. Potters call clay that's completely dry, *bone dry*. Bone-dry clay will be very light in color, and hard and chalky when you touch it.

Any clay creation that hasn't been fired yet is called *greenware*. When the greenware is bone dry, it's time to fire it in the kiln for the first time. This is called the *bisque* firing. It gets the clay hot enough that the silica starts to melt, making the clay hard. The clay pieces are now called *bisqueware*, and they're ready to be decorated with a special kind of paint called a *glaze*.

How Does Clay Get Hard?

If you've ever made something from real clay before, you know that once the clay dries out it can break very easily. And if you put water in it, it turns back to mush! So how did that mug you drink from get so hard? Clay can only get hard when it's heated to a very high temperature. Inside the clay are many pieces of tiny, sand-like particles called *silica*. Glass is another material that's made of silica. When the silica in the clay gets very hot, it melts, and as it cools, it becomes hard, like glass. Now the clay piece can hold water!

A glaze is a hard, glassy coating that goes over your bisqued work. Glazes are made from powdered glass (silica) and other ingredients that are mixed with water. They're easy to use because they come in jars. Paint them on your bisqueware, or dip the bisqued piece into the glaze. As the glaze dries, it will get powdery looking.

When the bisqueware has been glazed, you're ready to fire it in the kiln one last time (remember that the silica in the glaze needs high heat to turn it glassy looking). These glazed pots are now fired to an even hotter temperature than the bisque firing. As they get very hot, the powdery glazes start to melt and make a hard, smooth, colorful coating on the clay. This second firing in the kiln is called the *glaze firing*. After this firing, cups, bowls, or sculptures you made are now finished. Potters call their finished, glazed creations

ceramics. They're hard and durable, so you can eat or drink from them, or just show off your beautiful pieces to all your friends.

Setting Up Your Studio

Are you ready to get started? Then it's time to set up your own pottery studio with the tools and supplies you'll need.

Finding a Workspace

A studio is a place where you can create great works of ceramic art undisturbed by homework or your little brother or sister. A good place to make into a studio is the garage, a back porch, or a corner of the basement. Keep your clay work out of the kitchen—food and clay don't mix! You'll want a good sturdy worktable and a comfortable chair. If there isn't a sink nearby, have a big bucket of water and a sponge handy for cleanup.

Note to Parents and Teachers about Firing

If you don't have access to a kiln, you'll need to find a place that will fire the child's projects. Quite often the ceramic supply store where you buy the clay will fire projects for you, or direct you to a local potter with a kiln. Usually, they charge a small fee based on how much space the projects take up in the kiln.

Many cities and towns also have ceramic hobby shops where people paint their own glaze designs on ready-made ceramic pieces. These shops might also fire projects for a small fee.

Other places to inquire include local colleges, schools, or recreation facilities. Or try looking in the phone book under ceramics or pottery.

Note to Parents and Teachers about Dust Control

Controlling clay dust is a problem which all potters should address. Luckily, when working on a small scale with a bag or two of clay, dust is easily controlled. All clay contains silica which, in its dry state, can be harmful to the lungs if breathed in on a regular basis. There are several things you can do to reduce these associated risks.

The best way to avoid clay dust is to always keep the clay moist. Make sure kids have a spray bottle handy to keep clay scraps misted while they're working. Get the scraps back into a plastic bag as soon as possible. After projects are completed, kids should always wipe off work surfaces with a damp sponge—never sweep! Have kids change out of their clothes if they have a lot of dried clay on them, or have them wear a work smock. Remember, kitchen tables aren't a good place for clay projects. Likewise, keep food and drinks out of the clay studio.

Things You Need to Work with Clay

Many of the tools you'll need can be found around the house. Others you can make yourself. Still others you'll need to buy at a ceramic supply store. If you want to build up your tool supply gradually, just look at the beginning of a project you like. There you'll find a list of materials you need for each project. Some lists will be longer than others, depending on the project.

Stuff You Should Buy

You can find your clay and glazes at a ceramic supply store.

Earthenware Clay

Start with a 25-pound (11.4 kg) bag of white or reddish-brown earthenware clay. Either will do. Clays are rated with numbers called *cones*, which tell potters how hot to fire it. Earthenware clays are rated from cone 06 to 04.

Pin Tool

This is a wonderful, all-purpose clay tool. With it, you can cut and score the clay, or use it to scratch different textures into the clay. Remember that a pin tool is sharp. Be careful, and don't use it on anything except clay!

Low-fire Glaze

Glazes are used to decorate the surface of bisqued pottery. Glazes contain tiny bits of silica, which bonds with the clay and turns to glass when it's heated. Glazes melt at different temperatures and are generally grouped as either *high fire* or *low fire*. Low-fire glaze comes in a variety of colors and is painted on bisque-fired earthenware clay. Like clay, glaze is rated by cones to show the firing temperature. The label on the glaze jar should read *cone 06–04*. Make

Low-fire Underglaze

An underglaze is a colored stain that can be painted on greenware or bisqueware. Underglaze colors are crisper and won't blend together the way regular glaze will. Underglaze has no glasslike material in it, so if you want a smooth, glossy coating on your fired piece, you'll need to paint a clear glaze over it. Like glaze, underglaze should also be nontoxic, lead-free, and marked cone 06–04.

Clear Overglaze

This is a clear coat of glaze, usually painted on and fired after using an underglaze. Make sure it's nontoxic, lead-free, and marked cone 06-04.

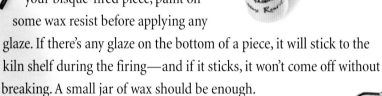

Paintbrushes

Buy small brushes for details like eyes and toenails, and bigger brushes to cover larger areas.

Liquid Wax Resist

To keep the glaze off the bottom of your bisque-fired piece, paint on some wax resist before applying any glaze. If there's any glaze on the bottom of a piece, it will stick to the kiln shelf during the firing—and if it sticks, it won't come off without breaking. A small jar of wax should be enough.

Dipping Tongs

If you plan to dip your creations into a bucket of glaze, you'll need dipping tongs, so the glaze won't get on your hands.

Note to Parents and Teachers about Clay

The best kind of clay for kids to use is low-fire earthenware clay. This is the type of clay most schools and summer camps use. Earthenware clays fire to a lower temperature than other types of clays, which makes them slightly more economical. Most important, though, earthenware clays are compatible with nontoxic, low-fire commercial glazes that can be purchased in jars at ceramic supply shops.

These glazes are labeled by the American Society for Testing Materials, so you can check the label to make sure they're nontoxic. Both the clay and glazes fire to cone 06-04. The cone number, designated by the symbol Δ, is simply a way potters indicate the firing temperature.

Stuff from around the House

These cool tools are easy to find.

Rolling Pin

This is used for rolling out slabs of clay like pie dough. You might find one in the kitchen you could use, but be sure to ask permission! Once you've used it for clay, don't use it for pie ever again.

Kitchen or Bathroom Scales

Some projects will tell you to start with a certain amount of clay—say, 1 or 2 pounds (.45 to .9 kg) of clay. Kitchen or bathroom scales will help you weigh out correct amounts. The bathroom scales aren't as accurate as kitchen scales, but that's okay. You only need to have a rough idea of how much the clay weighs for these projects. An easy way to start with the right amount of clay is to use a piece the size of a common object, like an egg or an apple. So start guessing how big your cat's head is!

Fork

An old kitchen fork is good for scoring or making textures in the clay. Don't use it in the kitchen after you use it on clay.

Vinegar

A little dab of plain white vinegar, mixed with a small amount of water, works like glue when joining pieces of clay.

Bowl and a Small Sponge

Use the sponge to dab on some vinegar and water to stick together two pieces of clay.

Wooden Craft Sticks

Wooden craft sticks (the kind in ice cream treats) are great for sculpting and smoothing the clay—especially in those hard-to-reach places where fingers won't fit. Start saving them up!

Ruler

Use a ruler to cut straight lines and to measure slab pieces.

Old Credit Card

Any old plastic card will do. They're great for smoothing and scraping the clay.

Spray Bottle

You might have an old pump spray bottle in your house that you can fill with water to mist the clay with if it gets too dry.

Hair Dryer

A hair dryer works well for drying the clay when it's too wet and soft to hold the shape you want. Of course, you'll only want to dry the clay a little bit, since clay that's too dry will crack when you try to shape it. Five minutes with the dryer is usually enough time to get the extra water out of clay that's very wet and soft.

Plastic Wrap or Plastic Dry-cleaner Bags

Cover your projects tightly with plastic if you want them to stay moist, so you can work on them later.

Bowls and Platters

Smooth, plastic containers, like plastic salad bowls from the grocery store, are good for press-molding projects.

Tubes and Cylinders

A cylinder is a tube-shaped object, like a can or a glass. These will come in handy for some of the projects. Save the cardboard tubes that come inside rolls of paper towels. You'll need them for some of the projects. You'll also need some large food cans, like the kind that juice and coffee come in. Number 10 cans are really big food cans (canned tomatoes often come in big number 10 cans). Save one or two empty ones. If you don't have any number 10 cans at home, ask for some in the kitchen of your school cafeteria.

Newspaper

You'll use newspaper in many of the projects to support the clay or to keep it from sticking to the number 10 cans or the cardboard tubes. It's also good to have newspaper to put under your projects when you're glazing them.

Big Bucket and Sponge

Use these to clean your work area of any dried clay when you're done. I like the kind of sponge you'd use to wash your Dad's car.

Tools You Can Make

Yes, you can make your own cool clay tools!

Cutoff Tool

This tool is used to slice smaller chunks of clay from your big block of clay. (It sounds sharp but it isn't, because the clay is so soft.) You can buy a cut-off tool at a ceramic supply store, or you can make your own with two wooden craft sticks and a piece of string. Here's how:

1. Use a pencil to make a mark across the middle of each wooden stick.

2. Use a butter knife to saw a small notch in the top and bottom edge of each stick where you made the pencil mark.

3. Cut a piece of string 10 inches (25.4 cm) long.

4. Wrap the end of the string into the notches you made on one of the sticks, and tie it tightly.

5. Wrap the other end of the string into the notches on the second stick, and tie it tightly. Make sure you have at least 8 inches (20.3 cm) of string left between the two sticks.

6. The sticks work as handles, and the notches keep the string from sliding.

Canvas Work Board

Whenever you roll out slabs of clay, you'll need to do it on a canvas-covered board to keep the clay from sticking. This board is also good for moving and storing projects. To make one, you'll need a piece of plywood 24 x 24 inches (61 x 61 cm) and a piece of canvas a little bit bigger than that. You can buy canvas at an art supply store or a fabric shop. Lay the canvas on a table, and put the board on top of it. Pull the edges of the canvas around the sides of the board, and tape it securely (kind of like wrapping a birthday present). Make sure you pull the canvas as tightly as you can so there are no wrinkles. Sometimes an extra pair of hands helps to get it really tight.

Wooden Slats

Two thin, wooden slats help keep the clay an even thickness when you roll it out with a rolling pin. Each slat should be $1/2$ inch (1.3 cm) thick, 1 to 2 inches (2.5 to 5 cm) wide, and 12 to 24 inches (30.5 to 61 cm) long.

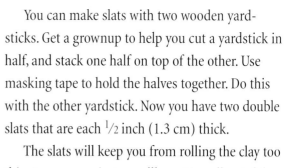

You can make slats with two wooden yardsticks. Get a grownup to help you cut a yardstick in half, and stack one half on top of the other. Use masking tape to hold the halves together. Do this with the other yardstick. Now you have two double slats that are each $1/2$ inch (1.3 cm) thick.

The slats will keep you from rolling the clay too thin. In some projects, you'll want to roll out slabs that are $1/4$ inch (6 mm) thick. Then just take off the tape from one double slat, and use the single slats instead of two together. You can still use the yardstick slats to measure with, too.

The Way to Use Clay

Now that you have your bag of clay, let's get to know it. You can do some amazing things with clay, but first you should understand how to work with it. Here are some important things to remember that will help you when you make the projects in this book.

Taking Care of Your Clay

The clay you buy from a ceramic supply shop will look like a big, wet brick wrapped in a plastic bag. Press your finger against the bag and the clay inside will feel soft. To keep it nice and soft, the clay must stay moist. Be careful not to poke or tear a hole in the plastic bag. If you do, the clay inside will quickly start to dry out and become hard. When you store your clay between projects, make sure you close the plastic bag tightly so it won't dry out.

Using the Cutoff Tool

When you're ready to get some clay for a project, open the plastic bag and peel it down part of the way. Hold your string cutoff tool by the wooden handles. Start from the back side of the block of clay. Pull the string tight, cutting into the clay, and pulling towards you. Cutting the clay like this will give you a nice, smooth chunk to work with.

Of course, it takes practice to cut off just the right amount of clay. If you didn't cut off enough clay for a certain project the first time, cut off another chunk, and slap the two chunks firmly together. You don't need to wedge fresh clay right out of the bag (there's more about wedging on page 21).

Whoops! What if you cut off way too much clay? If the project calls for a piece of clay the size of an apple, and you sliced off enough for a watermelon, recut the too-big piece and put some back in the plastic bag. If you're using a scale, check the

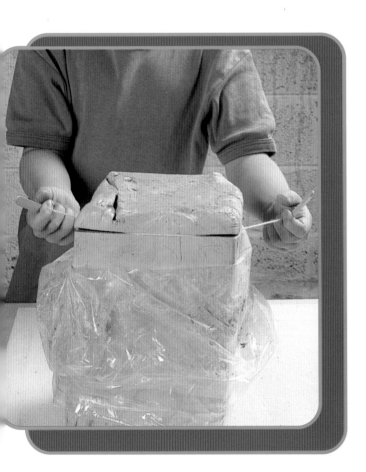

weight of the clay. If it's too heavy, slice pieces off the chunk and put them back in the plastic bag until you have the correct weight. Be sure to close your clay bag once you have all the clay you need.

No Thick Pieces

It's very important that any clay piece you put in the kiln is completely dry. When clay is fired, any moisture left in the clay turns to steam. If there's too much steam, it can become trapped in the clay. When this happens, the steam can crack the clay open as it tries to escape.

A clay sculpture or pot that's very thick might look dry on the outside, but it can still be wet inside. Thick clay pieces are very likely to crack open when they're fired. To keep this from happening, make sure your clay work is no thicker than 1 inch (2.5 cm). If, for example, you're adding a head on a dragon and it seems very large and thick, use your finger to hollow it out first. Then poke a small hole in it with the pin tool, to help the moisture escape. You can make the hole in a hidden place underneath the head if you don't want it to show.

Scoring and Sealing

You might want to join a handle on a mug, two sides of a box, or a head on an animal bank. There are two special ways of doing this, called *scoring* and *sealing*. Scoring means to scratch the clay with a pin tool or fork (see photos 1 and 2). Scratching the clay helps keep the two pieces from sliding apart. It's kind of like making sandpaper out of clay. If you've ever run your hand over a piece of sandpaper, you've probably noticed how it grabs and holds at your hand. Whatever the job, if you want it to stay, first score the clay where it will be joined to another piece.

Now you need something that acts like glue to help seal, or hold two pieces together. Mix 1 tablespoon (15 mL) of vinegar and 4 ounces (120 mL) of

water in a small bowl. Use a sponge to dab a little of this mixture onto the places where you scored the clay. Be sure to add just a little vinegar and water to the scored places. Too much water makes the clay feel sticky, and it's hard to make anything with clay that sticks to your fingers.

Some potters use a mixture of clay and water, called *slurry*, instead. To make slurry, mix a handful of clay in a bowl with a little water. Stir until it feels like pancake batter. To use slurry, just dab a very little bit onto the scored places. Too much slurry can make the clay too soft.

After you score and join the two pieces of clay, it's time to seal the joint. At first, you'll see a line or seam where the two pieces of clay meet. Use your finger or a wooden craft stick to blend the clay together until you can't see a line anymore (see photo 3).

Tired Clay

Yes, clay gets tired, too. When clay has been worked in your hands for a long time, tiny cracks begin to show as it starts to dry out. This happens because your hands actually pull the moisture out of the clay. When clay gets tired like this, mist it with water, then smooth the cracks out with a plastic card. If the cracks still won't go away, cover the project tightly with plastic wrap and let it rest for a while. Sometimes a little nap will do wonders! This gives the clay a chance to reabsorb some moisture so that you can work with it again.

Using the Hair Dryer

When you sculpt and form clay shapes, it's important that the clay feels soft and moist, and that it bends easily without cracking. Clay that you're sculpting should never be so wet that it's sticky, or so dry that it cracks.

Sometimes, though, a potter likes to *stiffen* the clay so that it will hold a particular shape. To stiffen the clay means to dry it slightly. For example, to make a clay box, stiffen the rectangular sides of the box before you put them together. Otherwise, the sides will sag, and your box will look warped.

A quick way to stiffen a clay project is to dry it with a hair dryer. Put the dryer on a medium setting and hold it 6 or 7 inches (15.2 to 17.8 cm) from the clay project. Keep moving the dryer from place to place on the project, always keeping a distance of 6 or 7 inches (15.2 to 17.8 cm). As soon as the clay is stiff enough to hold its shape, stop the dryer; it shouldn't take more than five minutes. Stiff clay still bends, but it feels a little harder—like shoe leather.

Wedging

As your projects take shape, you'll have a lot of scraps and lumps of unused clay collecting on your worktable. If you keep these scraps moist and put them back in a plastic bag, you'll be able to use them for another project. First, though, you'll have to *wedge* the pieces together. Wedging means to knead the clay with your hands to soften it and to remove air pockets. To keep it from sticking, always wedge the clay on a cloth-covered board. If the clay seems dry, mist it with water as you work. Now comes the fun part! Here's your chance to really give that clay a workout. Slam the clay down hard on the board about 10 times. Try to slam it down on a different side each time, so that it forms a cube shape. Now your old clay is ready to use again.

How to Use This Book

Now you're ready to get started. Look through the book and find a project that looks like fun. The list at the start of each project tells you what tools and how much clay you'll need. After you've made the project and it's bisque fired, pick out some great glaze colors, and follow the instructions for glazing and firing on pages 116 through 123.

Handbuilding Projects

Handbuilding means to make something out of clay without using a potter's wheel. Our own hands are by far the best tools for making things from clay, and this has been true for a very long time.

Pretend for a moment that you're living somewhere on our planet a thousand years ago. You find a vein of clay in a riverbank and decide to make a cup out of it. How would you do it? One way would be to roll the clay into a ball, then stick your thumb in it and pinch the sides to thin them. Or you could roll pieces of clay between your hands to make ropes of clay. Then you could stack the clay ropes in a circle, one on top of the other, to make a cup. You could also flatten the clay between your hands, then press it over a smooth, round, river rock to form a cup.

Today, we call these three ways of handbuilding *pinch, coil,* and *slab* construction. These basic skills haven't changed much over time, except that you'll be using a rolling pin to flatten slabs of clay. In the following projects, you'll learn how to make a pinch pot, how to roll out and stack coils, and how to flatten clay into slabs. You'll see all the different clay creations you can make with pinch pots and coils, starting with a simple

Pinched Bowl. From there, you can try your hand at making Animal Banks and Peruvian Stirrup Cups.

The slab projects start out simple, like the Secret Note Clay Pocket. Then you'll learn how much more you can do with slabs when you press mold a Mad Hatter Teapot, or use a balloon to help you make a Fantastical Dragon. You'll create a Glowing Lantern House with a cylinder, then go on to put together a really fun slab construction, such as the Mystical Wizard. You'll use these skills to make many different kinds of clay projects. So start exploring and see what you can do with clay!

Note: in all of the projects, using scales to weigh out the clay is optional. if you don't want to use scales, each project also uses common objects to describe how much clay you need. For example, you might need a piece of clay the size of an apple, or the size of a grapefruit.

How to Roll Out a Ball of Clay

Cut off a chunk of clay about the size of your hand. Squeeze the clay between your two cupped hands to start forming it into a rounded shape. Using one hand, roll the clay in a circular motion on the canvas work board (see photo 1). Keep rolling the clay in circles until you have a smooth, round ball. In the first project, you'll learn how to turn this ball into a pinch pot.

How to Roll Out a Coil

For a coil, cut off a piece of clay that will just fit in your cupped hand. Squeeze it gently in one hand so that it gets a little longer. Be careful not to squeeze too hard, or your fingers will make bumps in the clay. Place the clay on the cloth work board. With one hand, roll the clay back and forth in long, even strokes (see photo 2). It's better to use one hand instead of two hands. Two hands moving at different speeds will cause the coil to twist and break. As you work, move your hand to where the coil is too thick, and gently roll it back and forth to thin it out. Keep working the thick spots out until you have a nice, even coil. If the coil feels dry while you're rolling it out, dampen it with the spray bottle or a sponge.

Pinch & Coil

You'll use pinch pots in combination with coils to make the projects in this section. Before you start, practice rolling out balls of clay and coils, or ropes, of clay. To make a pinch pot, always start with a nice, round ball.

Pinched Bowl

A pinched bowl is really a cup without a handle. It's just the right size to fit comfortably in your hand while sipping orange juice. Making a pinched bowl is a good way to get the feel of clay. You'll make a simple pinch pot, then add a "foot." This design looks just like the tea bowl used for hundreds of years by Japanese potters. Make more than one bowl, and you can even have a tea ceremony with your friends.

抹茶 茶碗

What You Need

½ pound (.23 kg) of clay
Scales (optional)
Cutoff tool
Canvas work board
Pin tool
Ruler
Vinegar and water
Small sponge

What to Do

1. Use the clay cutter to slice off ½ pound (.23 kg) of clay.

2. Roll the clay into a ball that's a little bigger than a golf ball. It should fit comfortably in the palm of your hand.

3. Hold the ball in one hand, and push the thumb from your other hand into the center of the ball.

4. Push your thumb straight down, until you can just feel it in the palm of your other hand (see photo 1). The hole is deep enough when there's about ¼ inch (6 mm) between your thumb and the palm of your hand. You can check the thickness by pushing a pin tool through the bottom. Put your finger on the pin tool where it enters the clay, then pull the pin tool out. Measure on a ruler how much of the pin tool went into the clay.

5. Starting at the bottom, pinch the clay between your thumb and fingers while you slowly turn the bowl with your other hand (see photo 2). Pinch and turn as you gradually work your way to the top. Watch how the walls grow taller as you work. As you pinch, push out a little with your thumb. That will give your bowl a nice round shape. Keep the opening small by putting only your thumb inside the bowl. If you put your whole hand inside, your tea bowl will turn into a flat plate. Take your time! You must never rush a good Japanese tea bowl. If

you feel impatient, try listening to some relaxing music while you work. Or imagine you're in a Japanese garden sipping tea with your friends.

6. When you're satisfied with your pot, and it seems smooth and comfortable to hold in your hand, set it upside down on the table. It's time to add the foot.

7. The Japanese always add a little rim, called the foot, to the bottom of their tea bowls. Adding a foot to your tea bowl gives it a nice finishing touch. For the foot, start with a piece of clay about the size of a large grape. On the canvas work board, roll the clay back and forth with one hand to make a coil as thick as a pencil and 3 inches (7.6 cm) long.

8. On the bottom of your tea bowl, use the pin tool to score a circle the size of a silver dollar. Dab a little vinegar and water on with the sponge.

9. Press the coil into the scored circle (see photo 3), and seal it with your finger. Pinch off any extra coil.

3

The Way of Tea

Since ancient times in Japan, people have shared friendship and a love of nature in the tea ceremony. The tea bowls they used long ago for this important ceremony were always handmade, not formed on a potter's wheel. The Japanese have always valued handmade tea bowls because they find beauty in simple objects. They also feel that they can sense the spirit of the potter whose hand formed it. The Tea Masters who perform the tea ceremonies spend years perfecting their craft, until they can provide the most simple and beautiful and gracious ceremony possible. Here is a poem by an ancient Japanese Tea Master:

> Many though there be
> Who with words or even hands
> Know the Way of Tea
> Few there are or none at all
> Who can serve it from the heart
>
> If you have one pot
> And can make your tea in it
> That will do quite well
> How much does he lack himself
> Who must have a lot of things?
>
> Sen-no Rikya (1521-1591 A.D.)

Clay Clue

What if my pinch pot is lumpy and uneven?
Cut off a new piece of clay, roll it into a round ball, and try again. It's better to use a new piece of clay, in case the old piece is "tired" (see page 20). This time, don't rush it. Make smaller turns as you gradually work your way to the top. Try to pinch the same way every time with the same amount of pressure. Remember to push the clay out a little with your thumb as you pinch.

Fancy Goblet

A goblet is a type of fancy cup that sits on a long stem. To make one, start with a pinch pot, then stack a tower of coils to make the stem. When your goblet is done, you can pretend to be a knight at King Arthur's court, dining at a royal feast.

What You Need

½ pound (.23 kg) of clay for the cup, plus another 1 pound (.45 kg) for the stem

Cutoff tool

Scales (optional)

Pin tool

Vinegar and water

Small sponge

Canvas work board

What To Do

1. Slice off ½ pound (.23 kg) of clay with the cutoff tool.

2. Roll the clay into a ball. It should be a little bigger than a golf ball.

3. Slice off another 1 pound (.45 kg) of clay, and set it aside for later.

4. With the small ball of clay, make a pinch pot (follow steps 3 through 5 in the directions for making the Pinched Bowl project on page 25).

5. When your pinch pot is done, set it upside down on the table.

6. Use the pin tool to score a circle about the size of a half dollar on the bottom of the pinch pot. Dab a little vinegar and water onto the place where you scored. This is where you'll add the stem.

7. Pinch off a small handful of clay from the extra clay you saved.

8. Roll this clay into a coil on the canvas work board. Make a coil 4 to 5 inches (10.2 to 12.7 cm) long and ½ inch (1.3 cm)

thick. A coil that's too skinny won't be strong enough to support the pinch pot.

9. Press the coil into the scored circle, then build the stem by winding the coil on top of itself (see photo 1). Score the top of the coil as you go, dabbing on vinegar and water before pressing it firmly onto itself.

10. Keep rolling out the coils of the same thickness and adding them on, until the stem is 3 to 4 inches (7.6 to 10.2 cm) tall. It's easier to work with several short coils than to try to roll out one long coil.

11. Gradually make wider circles with the coils as you get near the bottom of the stem. The bottom of the stem should be as wide as the pinch pot is at the top. To make sure it will stand without wobbling, turn the goblet over and set it on the stem.

12. When the goblet stands steady, you can add decorations. It's fun to roll little balls of clay for jewels. Score the pinch pot where you want to add them, and press them in well (see photo 2). You can also draw designs with the pin tool.

The Most Famous Goblet of All

Legend has it that King Arthur's Knights of the Round Table spent a good bit of their time searching for a very precious goblet called the Holy Grail. The Grail was thought to be the same simple goblet Jesus drank from at the Last Supper. According to legend, The Grail was thought to have been brought to England soon after Jesus' death. Was The Holy Grail ever found? No one knows for sure. The Grail and all the legends surrounding it are shrouded in mystery.

Clay Clue

My goblet wobbles. What do I do?
You may have to re-do the coils. Try making the whole stem a little wider, to better support the pinch pot.

Animal Pinch Pot

It's fun to turn pinch pots into animal pots of almost any kind: dogs, cats, elephants, rabbits, anteaters, aardvarks! Use your imagination, and make up your own animal.

Making this cat pinch pot will probably give you ideas for making other great animals.

What You Need

½ pound (.23 kg) of clay for the pinch pot and another ½ pound (.23 kg) for the animal features

Cutoff tool

Scales (optional)

Pin tool

Canvas work board

Craft stick

Vinegar and water

Small sponge

Ruler

What to Do

1. Cut off ½ pound (.23 kg) of clay with the cutoff tool. Roll it into a round ball. It should be about the size of a large egg.

2. Make a pinch pot by following steps 3 to 5 in the Pinched Bowl project on page 25.

3. Set the pinch pot upside down on the table. Score the bottom of the pinch pot in four places where you want to add legs. Dab on a little vinegar and water where you scored.

4. Cut another ½ pound (.23 kg) of clay off the big block of clay. Divide this clay into four pieces that are about the same size. It's okay if they're not exactly equal.

5. Roll these four pieces into coils on the canvas work board. Make the coils ½ inch (1.3 cm) thick and 1 to 2 inches (2.5 to 5 cm) long. These will be the cat's legs. Bend the bottoms of the legs to make paws.

6. Work with the pinch pot upside down. Score the top of each leg, then press them, one at a time, into the scored places on the bottom of the pinch pot. Seal each leg with your finger or a wooden craft stick as you add them, until all the legs are well attached (see photo 1).

7. Place the pot right side up on its new feet. Use the pin tool to draw claws into the paws (see photo 2).

8. Now for the face. Add a nose first. Remember that a cat's nose is long, not round. Score on the pinch pot where you want to put the nose, then dab on a little vinegar and water. Pinch off a little bit of clay for the nose, and shape it so that it's narrow at the top and fatter at the bottom. Press it into the pinch pot where you scored the clay, then seal it with the wooden craft stick. Use the pin tool to poke holes for nostrils.

9. To make eye sockets, press your finger into the pinch pot. Score the eye sockets and dab on some vinegar and water.

10. Roll two pea-sized balls of clay for the eyes, and press them in well where you scored the clay (see photo 3). Use a pin tool to draw the iris and pupil.

11. Score near the top of the pinch pot for the ears. Dab on some vinegar and water. Cat's ears look like triangles, so shape two little triangles out of clay, and press them in where you scored.

12. Roll out a coil $1/4$ inch (6 mm) thick for the tail. Score the clay where you want to add the tail, then press it in well. Be sure to curl the tail back against the body of the cat. If you leave the tail sticking straight out, it will probably break off. You can curl the tail back to make it like the handle of a cup if you want.

13. Use the pin tool to scratch in whiskers and fur texture. Draw the mouth with the pin tool. Add any other details you want, such as teeth, or stripes if you want your cat to be a tabby.

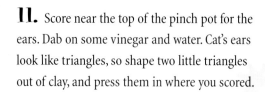

Animal Art Masterpieces

For as long as there have been artists, there have been animals to inspire them in their art. When the first cave person decided to decorate the walls of the cave, what did he or she draw? Animals, of course! A very famous cave in Lascaux, France, shows over 600 incredible paintings of bison, reindeer, and horses, all galloping in every direction over the walls and ceiling of the cave. The prehistoric artists who created these masterpieces were very advanced in their ability to create a sense of depth and perspective in their paintings. Many of the techniques they used wouldn't be used by artists again for thousands and thousands of years. This animal art was truly ahead of its time!

Animal Bank

Need a place to keep your spare change? Make a clay bank! Everyone's heard of a piggy bank. Pigs are great, but it's fun to make banks in the shapes of other animals, too. Here's how to make an alligator bank.

What You Need

1 ½ pounds (.68 kg) of clay for the body
and another ½ pound (.23 kg) for the
alligator features

Cutoff tool

Scales (optional)

Newspaper

Pin tool

Vinegar and water

Small sponge

Craft stick

Plastic card

Canvas work board

Ruler

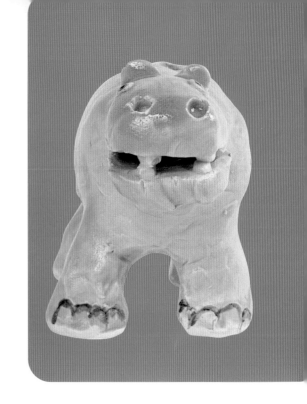

What to Do

1. Cut off two pieces of clay that are ¾ pound (.34 kg) each. Each piece will be about the size of a small apple. Roll them into balls.

2. Make a pinch pot from each ball, following steps 3 through 5 in the Pinched Bowl project on page 25.

3. Tear off two letter-sized pieces of newspaper and crumple them into balls. Stuff the newspaper inside each of the two pinch pots (see photo 1).

4. Score with the pin tool all around the top of one of the pinch pots. Dab on a little vinegar and water where you scored.

5. Now widen the opening of the other pinch pot by pinching and stretching it with your fingers, so that the rim of the first pinch pot fits partway inside it. The idea is to fit the two pinch pots together to make one hollow ball. Fitting one pinch pot slightly inside the other will leave a rim of clay where the pots' rims overlap.

6. Fit the two pinch pots together, rim to rim, so that the smaller one is slightly inside the larger one. Use your thumb to smear the rim of clay from the larger pinch pot into the smaller one (see photo 2). The crumpled newspaper inside them will keep the pots from collapsing as you work.

7. Use a plastic card to finish smoothing the clay until no seam is visible. You'll now have a large hollow ball about the size of a tennis ball. If you're wondering how to get the newspaper out, don't worry. The newspaper will burn up when the piece is fired in the kiln.

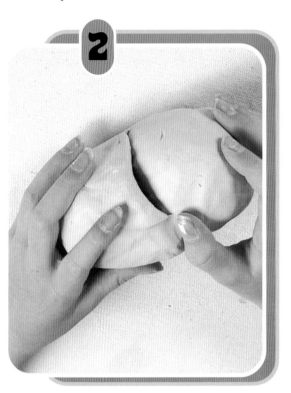

8. For an alligator, you'll need to make this round ball into a longer shape. Gently roll it back and forth on the canvas work board, rolling it into a longer, narrower shape (see photo 3).

9. To make the alligator's snout, pinch one end of the form, then gently pull on it (see photo 4).

10. For the legs, start with four pieces of clay the size of large grapes. Roll each piece into a thick, short coil. Bend the bottoms to make feet.

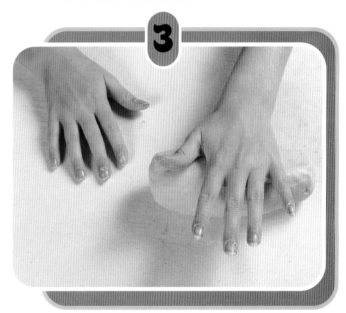

11. With the pin tool, score on the bottom of the alligator where you want to add legs. Dab on vinegar and water. Firmly press each leg into the clay where you scored, and seal them with a craft stick as you go.

12. Place the alligator on its feet. Use the pin tool to cut claws in the feet.

13. Now make the tail. Roll out another coil 1 to 2 inches (2.5 to 5 cm) long and $1/2$ inch (1.3 cm) thick. Make this coil taper to a point at one end. Score, dab on vinegar, and add the tail. The tail will be fairly short and stout. Long, skinny tails tend to break.

14. Push into the snout end with your fingers to make eye sockets, then score the clay and add clay eyeballs. To make a mouth, cut the snout open with the pin tool, then press in tiny pieces of clay for the teeth (see photo 5). Instead of scoring for such small pieces, just press them in well, and they'll usually stay. Poke holes with the pin tool for nostrils.

15. You can make scale patterns in many different ways. Try pressing in the round end of the pin tool. If you're really patient, flatten tiny, round pieces of clay, and press them into the body.

16. The last step is to use the pin tool to cut a slot for the coins in the top of the bank (see photo 6). If you make it large enough to shake the coins out, you won't have to break the bank to get your money. A good size is $^{1}/_{2}$ inch wide and 2 inches long (1.3 x 5 cm). That may seem too large, but it will be a little smaller after the bank is finished, because clay shrinks a little when it's fired.

Why Pigs?

In the Middle Ages, long before banks and teller machines, people kept their money in jars made from a type of clay called *pygg*. Over time, not only the name but the shape of the jar itself became a pig. It made sense since, for many hardworking peasants, their most valuable asset was the family pig.

Clay Clue

What should I do if I don't like how I cut the mouth?

Dab a little vinegar and water into the cut, then use a wooden craft stick to seal it closed, and try again.

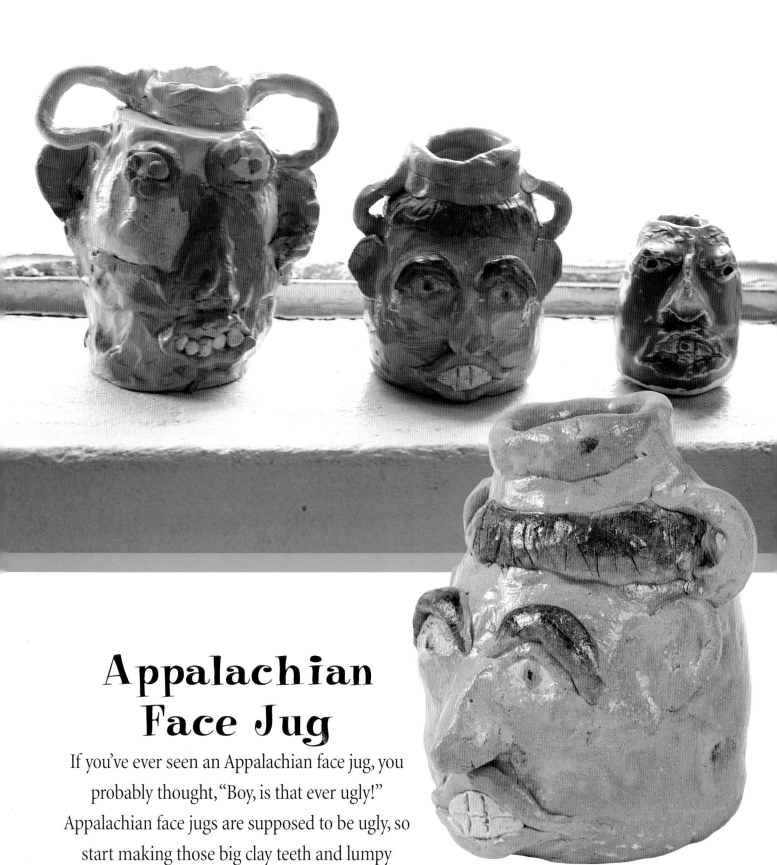

Appalachian Face Jug

If you've ever seen an Appalachian face jug, you probably thought, "Boy, is that ever ugly!" Appalachian face jugs are supposed to be ugly, so start making those big clay teeth and lumpy noses. The uglier, the better!

What You Need

Two pieces of clay, 2 pounds each (.9 kg) and another pound (.45 kg) for the face, handles, and top of the jug

Cutoff tool

Scales (optional)

Canvas work board

Newspaper

Plastic card

Pin tool

Hair dryer

Ruler

Wooden craft stick

Small bowl of vinegar and water

Small sponge

What to Do

1. Slice off two pieces of clay with the cutoff tool that are 2 pounds (.9 kg) each. Roll them into two balls on the canvas work board. They should be about the size of large oranges.

2. Make two pinch pots by following the directions from the Pinched Bowl project (use steps 3 through 5 on page 25).

3. Connect the two pinch pots together by following steps 3 through 7 from the Animal Bank project (see pages 34—35). You'll need to use a little more newspaper since these pinch pots are bigger.

4. Once the pinch pots are joined together with newspaper wads inside, smooth the clay all over with the plastic card. Roll the ball gently on the canvas work board to get it round.

5. Set the big, hollow ball of clay on one end on the table. Gently tap it on the table to flatten the bottom (see photo 1). Keep tapping, until the bottom is flat and the ball will stand still without rocking or tipping.

6. Use the pin tool to cut a round hole in the top of the ball 2 inches (5 cm) wide (see photo 2). Score around the opening. If the clay seems soft and bends in easily when you score, use a hair dryer for five minutes to stiffen it, until you can score the ball without it sagging in.

7. Pinch off a handful of clay the size of a plum, and roll it into a short, thick coil on the work board. (See page 23 if you need help rolling out a coil.)

8. Place the coil around the hole you cut, and press it in firmly. Seal it with the wooden craft stick. This will make the top of the jug. Add one or two more coils to make the top higher, but be sure to score the top of each coil before you add another one, and firmly press in each one (see photo 3).

9. If you want handles on your face jug, make two more coils. Score the clay at the top rim of the jug, then score it again 3 inches (7.6 cm) below that. Dab on vinegar and water, then press the coils in and seal the seams.

10. Now for the face. Score near the center of the face where you want to add a nose. Remember that a real nose is shaped sort of like a triangle, not round like an apple. Press the nose in, and seal it well. Make nostrils by pressing the round end of the pin tool into the clay.

11. Make round balls the size of grapes for eyes. Score the clay, dab on vinegar and water, and press them in well. Use the pin tool to draw details in the eyes.

12. Roll out more coils for the lips and eyebrows. Flatten little pieces of clay for teeth (see photo 4). Contrast the brown clay by using white clay, if you have some, for teeth. Remember to score whenever you add anything. Dab on a little vinegar and water, too, for extra holding power.

Jugs, Mountains & Moonshine

Back in the mountains of Appalachia, in the days of your great, great grandparents, everyone kept their food in pottery jugs. (Plastic containers hadn't been invented yet!) Face jugs were particularly good for keeping Great-Great-Grandpa's moonshine in—probably because after one sip he looked something like the face on the jug!

Legend has it that face jugs were also put on the graves of people after they died. Family members kept an anxious eye on the jug. If it cracked before a year went by, that meant Grandpa's spirit was wrestling the devil!

Peruvian Stirrup Cup

Have you ever wondered what people used before plastic sports bottles were invented? Stirrup cups from ancient Peru were usually made in the shape of an animal or person. You can make one like this parrot, or come up with your own design. Maybe a llama would be nice.

What You Need

2 pounds of clay (.9 kg) for the cup and
 another 1 pound (.45 kg) for the handle
Scales (optional)
Cutoff tool
Pin tool
Newspaper
Vinegar and water
Craft stick
Plastic card
Canvas work board
Rolling pin
¼-inch (6 mm) wooden slats
Ruler
Hair dryer

What to Do

1. Cut off two pieces of clay that are 1 pound (.45 kg) each. Roll the two pieces into round balls. They'll be the size of apples.

2. Make two pinch pots from the round balls. Go back to the Pinched Bowl project on page 25 for directions on making a pinch pot.

3. Connect the two pinch pots, following steps 3 through 7 from the Animal Bank project on pages 34—35. Now you should have a hollow ball about the size and shape of a large baking potato.

4. Set the hollow ball on one end, and flatten the bottom by gently tapping it on the table, so it will stand without rocking.

5. Gently squeeze the hollow ball 1 to 2 inches (2.5 to 5 cm) from the top (see photo 1). This forms the parrot's neck.

6. Scrape and smooth the clay all over with the plastic card. This parrot should have a round, smooth body with a small round head.

7. Pinch off a little extra clay for the beak. A parrot's beak is fairly large and it curves downward. The beak should be almost as big as the head. Score the head where you want to add the beak, and dab on vinegar and water. Press the beak in well, and seal it with your finger or a craft stick.

8. Roll two little balls for the eyes. Score the clay and press them in well. Use the pin tool to poke holes for the pupils. Also, poke little holes for nostrils in the beak.

9. Draw on some wings with the pin tool, or wait until later and paint the wings on with glazes or underglazes.

10. For the handle, cut off another 1 pound (.45 kg) of clay. Throw this clay down hard on the canvas work board to flatten it. Flip it over, then throw it down again.

11. Use the rolling pin and a pair of ¼-inch (6 mm) wooden slats to flatten it. Turn to page 49 for more about how to roll a slab with slats.

12. Use the ruler and pin tool to cut a strip of clay 6 inches (15.2 cm) long and 2 inches (5 cm) wide (see photo 2). Save the extra slab pieces. You'll need them later.

13. Gently fold the sides of the strip over to make a hollow tube 6 inches (15.2 cm) long. Score the clay where the sides meet, then press them together. Keep one finger inside the tube while you're pressing so it will keep its shape.

14. Put one finger in either end of the tube, then gently bend the tube into a U shape (see photo 3).

15. Set the tube handle aside for the moment, and go back to the parrot. With a pin tool, cut a round hole the size of a quarter in the back of the parrot's head (see photo 4). Cut another quarter-sized hole 3 inches (7.6 cm) lower on the body, behind the parrot's wings. Score around both holes, and dab on a little vinegar and water. This is where you'll attach the hollow handle.

16. Pick up the hollow handle, and gently stretch the openings at either end so they're a little wider. Score around the holes in the parrot's head, dab on vinegar and water, then press one end of the tube over the top hole in the parrot's head, and the other end into the lower hole. Use a wooden craft stick to seal the handle.

17. Use the hair dryer to dry the handle for about five minutes (see photo 5). When you're done, the handle should be slightly stiff, but not completely dry.

18. Use the pin tool to cut a hole the size of a quarter in the back of the handle, 2 to 3 inches (5 to 7.6 cm) from the top. Score around the hole, and dab on some vinegar and water.

19. From the extra slab pieces, cut a strip 2 by 2 inches (5 x 5 cm). Score the edges. Make a short tube by bending the sides of the piece together, the way you did for the handle.

20. Gently stretch the opening of the tube a little bit at one end. Press the wider end of the tube over the hole at the back of the handle. Seal it with a craft stick (see photo 6). This will be the spout for the handle.

5

6

Have Llama, Will Travel

In the South American country of Peru, stirrup cups were made with a special handle that doubled as a pouring spout. These cups got their name because archaeologists thought the handle was shaped like a stirrup on a saddle. This clever design kept water from spilling out while it was being carried. It also made a handy place to tie the cup to the pack on a llama while the Peruvians traveled through the Andes Mountains.

Clay Clue
What if my tube starts to crack while I'm bending it?

Rub a little vinegar and water into the cracks, smooth the clay with a plastic card, and try again.

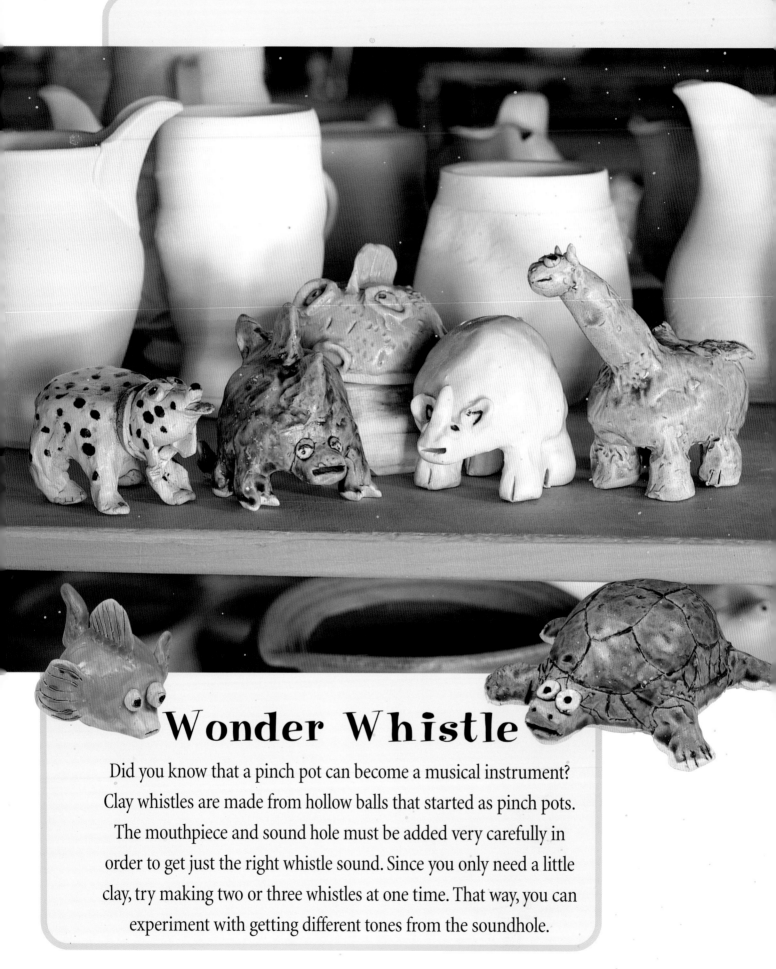

Wonder Whistle

Did you know that a pinch pot can become a musical instrument? Clay whistles are made from hollow balls that started as pinch pots. The mouthpiece and sound hole must be added very carefully in order to get just the right whistle sound. Since you only need a little clay, try making two or three whistles at one time. That way, you can experiment with getting different tones from the soundhole.

What You Need

1 pound (.45kg) of clay
(more, if you want to try
several whistles)

A sharpened, round pencil

Wooden craft stick

Fettling knife, or pocket knife (handle carefully!)

Damp sponge

Pin tool

What to Do

1. Start with a round ball of clay the size of a golf ball. Hold the ball in one hand, and push your thumb from the other hand into the center of the ball. Keep pushing until you can feel pressure from your thumb in the palm of your hand.

2. Pinch the clay between your thumb and forefingers. Pinch in circles, working your way up, so that you form a round pinch pot with a very small opening. The walls should be thin and even, not thick and lumpy.

3. When the walls are nicely thinned and even, pull your thumb out and pinch the opening closed (see photo 1). This takes practice and good control of the clay. If you need to, add a little piece of clay over the opening to close it off.

4. Tap the hollow ball lightly on the table to flatten the bottom of it.

5. Let your hollow ball harden a little before the next step. You can let it air dry for 20 to 25 minutes, or use the hair dryer for 5 minutes. The clay should

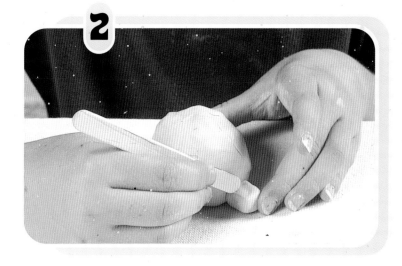

be stiff enough to hold its shape, but not so dry that it cracks when you press your finger against it.

6. The next step is to make a mouthpiece. Roll out a little coil of clay that's as thick as your finger and 1 inch (2.5 cm) long. With the pin tool, score a spot on the side of the hollow ball, just above the flattened bottom. Now add the mouthpiece so that it's on the same level as the flattened bottom. Seal the seam with your finger or the craft stick (see photo 2).

7. Make the sound hole in the flattened bottom, just behind the mouthpiece. Carefully push the pointed end of the pencil into the clay ball so that the pencil fits just inside the walls of the hollow ball, right behind the mouthpiece. The side of the pencil should be touching the inside wall of the hollow ball behind the mouthpiece (see photo 3). Push the eraser end of the pencil back towards the mouthpiece to widen the sound hole a little.

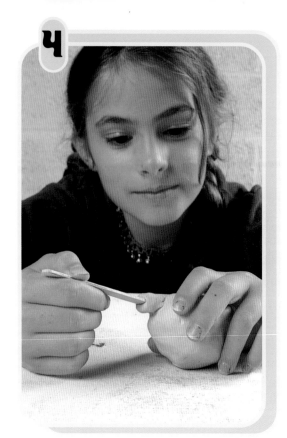

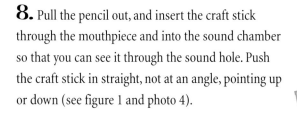

8. Pull the pencil out, and insert the craft stick through the mouthpiece and into the sound chamber so that you can see it through the sound hole. Push the craft stick in straight, not at an angle, pointing up or down (see figure 1 and photo 4).

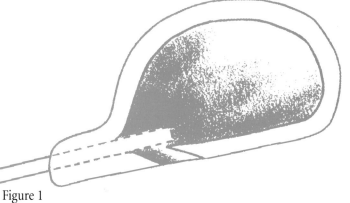

Figure 1

9. Use your fettling knife to carve a beveled edge on the side of the sound hole furthest from the mouthpiece (see photo 5 on page 47). Leave the craft stick in for now to support the clay while you cut the bevel. A bevel is a sharp, angled edge. When you blow into the mouthpiece, the air passing over the beveled edge makes the whistle sound.

46

10. After you cut the bevel into the sound hole, pull the craft stick out. Blow gently into the mouth-piece to see if it will whistle. If it doesn't, check all the holes to see that they're cut cleanly without any little clay crumbs blocking the air passages.

11. Once you get sound from your whistle, you can turn it into an animal, or some other type of figure. Be careful not to change or block the airways of the whistle when you add features.

Clay Clue

When I roll out my coil, it gets hard and flat.

Get a fresh piece of clay and try again. This time don't press down as hard as you roll it out. Take a damp sponge and run it over the coil now and then as you work to keep it soft. If you feel your coil start to flatten, gently tap the coil on the table where an edge is forming to round it out.

4

Simple Slab Projects

If you've ever rolled out pie dough, you can roll out a slab of clay. Once you've flattened a clay slab with the rolling pin, it's amazing how many different kinds of projects you can make just by cutting shapes from it. Tiles, coasters, puzzles, wind chimes, and chess or checkers game boards are just a few ideas for quick, easy-as-pie projects.

Later on, you'll learn how to press your slab into a mold, how to cut and build boxes and pyramids—even how to use a slab and a balloon to make a dragon!

How to Roll out a Slab

First, let's practice rolling out a big piece of clay into a slab. Slice off some clay, and form it into a ball that's somewhere between the size of a grapefruit and the size of a canteloupe.

To start flattening the clay, slam it down hard on the canvas-covered work board. Pick it up, flip it over, and slam it down again (see photos 1—3). Do this three or four times. Set the clay in the middle of the canvas work board, and place the wooden slats on either side of the clay. Some of the projects will need a ¹/₂-inch (1.3 cm) slab and others use a ¹/₄-inch (6 mm) slab. Remember that if you used a yardstick to make your slats, two stacked pieces will help you make a slab that's ¹/₂ inch (1.3 cm) thick. Single slats made from a yardstick are ¹/₄ inch (6 mm) thick. Roll back and forth over the clay with the rolling pin, until the clay is so flat that it rolls over the wooden slats, too (see photo 4, at left). Now you have an even slab that's just the right thickness. Some projects will need a circle-shaped slab. For a round slab, roll the pin in all directions, not just back and forth.

As you work, pay attention to where the slab is too thick, and roll it out more there. Don't press down too hard. It's better to work slowly with long, even strokes. You'll know you're done when the rolling pin rolls evenly over the clay and the slats without feeling bumpy.

Moon and Stars Wind Chime

Here's another way to make music with clay. This wind chime makes a nice sound when it blows in the wind. Or hang your moon and stars over your bed, so you can contemplate the universe while you relax.

What You Need

5 pounds (2.3 kg) of clay
Cutoff tool
Scales (optional)
Canvas work board
1/4-inch (6 mm) wooden slats
Star-shaped cookie cutters
Empty tin can
Pin tool
Wooden pencil
Ruler
String
Sturdy stick, 12 inches (30.5 cm) long

What to Do

1. Cut off 5 pounds (2.3 kg) of clay with the cutoff tool. A ball of clay this big should be about the size of a cantaloupe. You probably won't need this much, but it's a good idea to have a big slab to work with. Mist the extra slab pieces when you're done, and put them back in the plastic bag. You can wedge them and use them for another project.

2. Follow the directions on page 49 for rolling out a slab of clay. Use the 1/4-inch (6 mm) slats to get the right thickness.

3. Cut out four stars with the star-shaped cookie cutters (see photo 1). Remember, don't use Mom's cookie cutters in the kitchen after you've used them on clay.

4. To cut out a round moon, press the empty can into the slab. If you want a crescent moon, use your pin tool to cut this circle into a crescent.

5. Use the wooden pencil to poke a hole into the top of each shape (see photo 2). Clay shrinks a little when it's fired, so make the holes almost as wide as the pencil.

6. Set the moon and stars aside to dry. Put a book on top of the shapes so they'll dry flat. Lay a sheet of paper over them first, so the book won't get clay on it.

7. After you've glazed and fired the shapes, assemble the wind chimes. First, cut five pieces of string, each 8 to 10 inches (20.3 to 25.4 cm) long. Tie one end of each string securely to the stars and moon, then tie the other end of each string to the stick. Space them 2 to 3 inches (5 to 7.6 cm) apart so they'll touch each other when the wind blows.

8. Arrange the shapes evenly across the stick so that the wind chime is balanced. Now tie another string 12 inches (30.5 cm) long to either end of the stick so it forms a loop for hanging the wind chime.

Secret Note Clay Pocket

These super-secret notekeeper pockets are super easy to make. Hang one in a special place, like a tree. If a friend comes by when you're not home, the secret message will be waiting for you in your clay pocket.

What You Need

5 pounds (2.3 kg) clay
Cutoff tool
Scales (optional)
Canvas work board
½-inch (1.3 mm) wooden slats
Rolling pin
Pin tool
Plant cutting
Vinegar and water
Small sponge
Newspaper

What to Do

1. Use the cutoff tool to slice the 5 pounds (2.3kg) of clay roughly in half. You don't have to be exact.

2. With the rolling pin, roll out two slabs on the canvas work board. Use the ½-inch (1.3 cm) slats to get the right thickness. From the first slab, cut an oval shape (an oval is egg-shaped) that is 7 inches (17.8 cm) long (see photo 1).

3. Put the oval shape on the second slab. Trace and cut another oval shape the same size.

4. Cut one of the ovals in half.

5. Lay a plant cutting on one of the half ovals (see photo 2). Plants that are hard and tough, like pine needles or holly leaves, work best.

6. Use the rolling pin to gently roll the plant cutting into the clay (see photo 3).

7. Now remove the plant from the clay, and you'll see a plant imprint.

8. Place the half-oval with the plant imprint on top of the whole oval, so that they match at the bottom and look like a pocket.

9. Score all along the edges where the two slabs meet. Dab a little vinegar and water on the area you scored.

10. Crumple some newspaper, and tuck it inside the pocket so it sticks out a little (see photo 4).

11. Now firmly squeeze and pinch the slabs together.

12. With the pin tool, make a small hole at the top of your clay pocket so you can hang it on a nail after it's fired.

Taco Letter Holder

This letter holder is shaped like a taco, but don't stuff it with lettuce! Instead,
put it on your desk to hold notes or pen pal letters.

What You Need

3 pounds (1.4 kg) of clay

Cutoff tool

Rolling pin

½-inch (1.3 cm) wooden slats

Canvas work board

Disposable plastic salad bowl

Pin tool

Things to imprint, such as
   rubber stamps, plants, buttons,
   a paper doily

Wooden board, 1 inch (2.5 cm)
   wide and 8 to 10 inches (20.3 to
   25.4 cm) long

Vinegar and water

Small sponge

What to Do

1. Cut off 3 pounds (1.4 kg) of clay. This much clay should be about the size of a grapefruit.

2. Roll it into a slab on the canvas work board, using the rolling pin and the ½-inch (1.3 cm) slats.

3. Place the salad bowl upside down on the slab. Use the pin tool to cut a round circle by tracing around the bowl.

4. While the circle is still lying flat on the table, you can experiment with imprinting different textures into the clay (see photo 1). Try pressing a button into the clay, or a small seashell. You might press a round paper doily into the clay to make a lace design.

5. Once you've decorated the clay circle, gently fold it in half with the design on the outside. Now drape it over the edge of the wooden board (see photo 2). Check to see that the sides of the circle are even with each other. The circle is now shaped like a taco.

6. Use your pin tool to cut two small strips from your extra slab pieces. They should be about 2 x 2 inches (5 x 5 cm), but you don't need to be exact. These strips keep the holder standing upright once you take it off the board. Use the pin tool to score two evenly spaced places on the outer fold of the letter holder. Dab some vinegar and water there, then press the two clay strips into place (see photo 3).

7. Wait 15 to 20 minutes, until the clay has stiffened a little, then take the letter holder off the board. Set it on the table to see if it will stand steady on the two clay strips. Adjust the strips if you need to, then let the letter holder finish drying.

Clay Clue

What if I want to start my design over?

If the clay circle is still lying flat, just smooth over the old design with a plastic card, then try a new design.

If the clay has already stiffened, you must moisten, then wedge it before you roll it out again. See page 21 for more about wedging.

Press Molding

Press molding is a way of making ceramics by pressing soft slabs of clay into or over an object, using it as a mold. As the slab dries, it takes on the shape of the object. Start looking for interesting things to use as molds. Old bowls or platters work well.

Hanging Birdbath

Birds love to play in water as much as you do. Have you ever seen a bird pool party? Hang this bath in a tree, and the birds can party safely out of the family cat's reach.

What You Need

7 pounds (3.2 kg) of clay
Scales (optional)
Canvas work board
1/2-inch (1.3 cm) wooden slats
Rolling pin
Plastic wrap
Plastic garbage can lid
Pin tool
Vinegar and water
Small sponge
1/4-inch (6 mm) cord

What to Do

1. Slice 7 pounds (3.2 kg) off your block of clay. If you rolled it into a ball, it would be the size of a honeydew melon.

2. Follow the directions on page 49 for rolling out a slab. Use the 1/2-inch (1.3 cm) slats to help you get the slab even. Roll the rolling pin in all directions so that the slab is round, not long and narrow. You may have to move the slats to different parts of the slab as you work.

3. Line the inside of the garbage can lid with plastic wrap. Birds like a shallow bath, with the water only 1 to 2 inches (2.5 to 5 cm) deep. An upside-down garbage can lid is just deep enough.

4. Press the slab of clay inside the plastic-lined lid so it fits over the plastic wrap (see photo 1). The wrap will keep the clay from sticking to the lid.

5. Use the pin tool to trim the edges of the slab to get the shape you want. Try cutting the edge into a curve or rounded shape.

6. For the handles, pinch off three handfuls of clay the size of plums. On the work board, roll out three fat coils, each 3 inches (7.6 cm) long and 3/4 inch (1.9 cm) wide.

7. Bend the coils into circles. Now score on the birdbath in three places where you want to add the coil handles. Place them at equal distances apart around the edge so the birdbath will hang evenly (see photo 2). Dab on vinegar and water where you scored.

8. Press the coil handles firmly into the scored places.

9. Let the birdbath sit overnight in the lid to stiffen up before you take it out. After it's glazed and fired, tie some strong ¼-inch (6 mm) cord to the handles so that you can hang it up.

Clay Clue

How do I glaze such a big project?

Use the bucket method! Lay two wooden paint stirrers like a pair of railroad tracks across the top of the bucket. Hold one side of the birdbath up, so that it's at a slant, while the other edge rests on the slats. That way, the glaze will run back into the bucket. See page 119 for more about glazing this way.

Otis's Turtle

Otis looked closely at a turtle shell and decided to make his clay turtle even more lifelike by drawing in all the little plates and ridges. Now his turtle lives in the garden!

What You Need

3 pounds (1.4 kg) of clay for the top shell,
   2 pounds (.9 kg) for the bottom shell, and
   a little more for the head, feet, and tail

Cutoff tool

Scales (optional)

Canvas work board

1/2-inch (1.3 cm) wooden slats

Rolling pin

Disposable plastic salad bowl

Plastic wrap

Pin tool

Vinegar and water

Small sponge

Hair dryer

Pictures of turtles

What to Do

1. Cut off 2 pounds (1.4 kg) of clay and roll it into a slab. Use the 1/2-inch (1.3 cm) slats to get it to an even thickness all over (see page 49 for more about rolling slabs). Roll in all directions so the slab is shaped more or less like a circle.

2. Place the plastic salad bowl upside down on top of the slab. Use the bowl to trace around and cut a circle the same size as the bowl. This round slab will be the bottom of the shell. Set it aside for now.

3. Cut off another 3 pounds (1.4 kg) of clay and roll it into a slab, using the ¹/₂-inch (1.3 cm) slats. To make the slab into a circle shape, move the rolling pin in all directions.

4. Line the inside of a salad bowl with plastic wrap. Press the slab inside the bowl, over the wrap (see photo 1). The plastic wrap will keep the clay from sticking to the bowl. Trim off the extra clay with the pin tool. Set the bowl and slab aside for now, and go back to the first slab you made for the shell bottom.

5. Pinch off four pieces of clay the size of plums, and roll them into short, fat coils, each 2 inches (5 cm) long. These will be the turtle's feet. Score on the bottom slab in four places where you want to add feet. Dab on vinegar and water, and press the feet in well. Use the pin tool to draw or cut claws into the feet.

6. To make the bottom shell fit under the top shell, you'll need to roll the edges of the slab up slightly all around, except where the feet are (see photo 2). When you're done, the bottom slab will look like a shallow bowl with feet.

7. Pinch off another plum-sized piece of clay for the head. Shape it like a turtle's head. Look at your pictures of turtles if you need help. Score on the edge where you want to add the head, then dab on some vinegar and water, and press it in well. Roll little balls of clay for the eyes. Use the pin tool to cut into the clay for the mouth and to poke holes for the nostrils.

8. Roll out one more little coil for the tail. Score, dab on vinegar and water, and press it in well.

9. Go back to the slab you pressed into the bowl. This will be the top shell. Use a hair dryer for five minutes to stiffen the clay so it will hold its

shape when you take it out of the bowl. The clay should be slightly stiff, but still soft enough to bend without cracking.

10. Turn the bowl upside down on top of the bottom shell. Lift off the bowl, and the top shell willl pop out. You'll probably have to bend the shell a little, and adjust the feet and head slightly, to get a good fit. You can score, dab on vinegar and water, and press the shell in if

you want it stuck permanently to the bottom shell. If not, put some plastic wrap between the top shell and the bottom shell while it dries. That way, you'll have a turtle that doubles as a covered dish. You can even make a little bird, or some other animal, and press it into the top of the shell, and it will work as a handle.

11. Now it's time to decorate the shell. Look at pictures of turtles and examine the shell pattern. You can draw the same kind of pattern with the pin tool (see photo 3), or you can invent your own pattern.

3

Clay Clue

If you decide not to stick the top shell to the bottom one, be sure to glaze the top shell the same as you would the lid for a project. Use wax resist around the shell's bottom edge. Turn to page 117 for more about glazing a lidded project.

Fast Turtle Facts

* Turtles have been around for more than 230 million years—they were on Earth before the dinosaurs were!

* The largest turtle ever found was a leatherback sea turtle. It weighed 2,120 pounds (962.5 kg), and its shell was 9 feet 5 1/2 inches (2.84 m) long. The smallest turtle is the Bog Turtle, whose shell is under 4 inches (10.2 cm) long!

* Ever wonder how a turtle breathes? Because of its shell, it can't simply expand its chest like you do. Instead, a turtle has special muscles that move its internal organs around to make room for the air in its lungs.

* Turtles have excellent eyesight and can see in color! They are particularly sensitive to the colors red and yellow. Turtles also have a special organ, called the Jacobson's Organ, on the roof of their mouth. This organ gives turtles a super-strong sense of smell—even underwater! However, turtles have very tiny ears, which makes it hard for them to hear.

* Turtle shells are made of keratin, which is the same substance that makes up our hair and nails. Turtles can feel when someone is touching their shell.

* Turtles are the only reptiles without teeth.

* Turtles live longer than any other vertebrate. They can live for more than 100 years.

Mad Hatter Teapot

In Lewis Carroll's strange tale, Alice falls down a rabbit hole and enters a crazy world, where the Mad Hatter hosts a never ending tea party. Bats twinkle, tea trays float in the sky, and riddles have no answers. (Just why *is* a raven like a writing desk?) What sort of wacky logic can you use for a tea party where the guests are rabbits and mice, and no one has time to wash the dishes? Any way you do it, have a madly great time!

"We're all mad here. I'm mad. You're mad."
Cheshire Cat, *Alice in Wonderland*

What You Need

5 pounds (2.3 kg) of clay

Cutoff tool

Rolling pin

Wooden slats

Canvas work board

Pin tool

2 small bowls that are the
same size (disposable plastic
salad bowls will do)

Plastic wrap

Hair dryer

Vinegar and water

What To Do

1. Cut off 5 pounds (2.3 g) of clay. It will be the size of a canaloupe. Use the rolling pin and wooden slats to roll out a slab on the canvas work board.

2. Place one of the bowls upside down on the slab. Cut out two circles by tracing around the bowl twice with the pin tool (see photo 1), but make the circles a little bigger than the bowl. Save the extra slab pieces.

3. Line the two bowls with plastic wrap. Press the two slab circles inside the bowls. Use the hair dryer for five minutes or so, until the clay is slightly stiff.

4. Score the outer edges of the slab circles and dab on vinegar and water.

5. With the slabs still inside them, press the two bowls together (see photo 2). Take off the bowls. The clay should hold its shape, since you stiffened it slightly with the hair dryer. Pinch the rim together where the sides meet.

6. To make the lid, use the pin tool to cut a round hole in the top. Cut out another hole in the side for the spout.

7. Use your extra slab pieces to make a lid and handle. First, make the spout on this teapot by forming a tube shape from a strip of clay. Score around the hole you cut in the side of the teapot, dab on some vinegar and water, then fit the spout over the hole (see photo 3). Seal the seam with your finger.

8. From an extra slab piece, cut a round circle that is a little bigger than the hole you cut in the top of the teapot. This will be the lid. Roll out a coil 2 inches (5 cm) long, and add the coil to the inside of the lid, so that it just fits inside the hole (see photo 4). This design keeps the lid from sliding off.

Clay Clue

What if the clay in the bowls falls flat when I take it out?

Put the circles back into the bowls. Stiffen them with the hair dryer for a few more minutes. Dry the middles a little more than the edges.

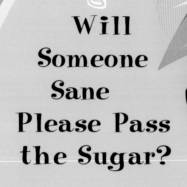

Will Someone Sane Please Pass the Sugar?

The Hatter in *Alice's Adventures in Wonderland* was so strange he wore a watch that told the day but not the hour. His best friend was a talking rabbit. They used a dormouse as a cushion. The Hatter criticized the way Alice said everything—even though he always knew exactly what she meant! Meanwhile, he didn't make much sense at all. Did you ever wonder about the hosts of the "Mad Tea Party," and why it was called that? It made sense to children who lived when Lewis Carroll did. (He's the one who wrote about Alice's adventures.)

You see, big felt hats—like the Hatter's—were very popular back then. They were made by soaking the felt in mercury. The hat makers (also called hatters or milliners) didn't know that handling mercury is dangerous! It causes tremors and twitches, trouble speaking, and unclear thinking. So hatters acted crazy—and "mad" was the word for that.

But that's only half the story! The Hatter's good friend was the March Hare. "Mad as a March hare" was a popular saying when Lewis Carroll was a boy. It meant hyperactive, in a silly way, like running around in circles or talking gibberish.

So, the first children to read *Alice's Adventures in Wonderland* knew that the Tea Party wasn't just mad—its hosts were, too!

Slabs & Balloons

Wow! How do balloons and clay go together? Simple. You'll drape pieces of clay over a blown-up balloon. This lets you make big, rounded clay shapes. After the clay stiffens, have fun popping the balloon with your pin tool.

Fantastical Dragon

Imagine a dragon, and you might picture a large, fire-breathing, reptilian monster! Or maybe your dragon is friendly, not fierce. This project is fun because you use a balloon to make the dragon. It will look all puffed up, ready to blow out some fire—or maybe it just ate too many cookies.

What You Need

5 pounds (2.3 kg) of clay for the body, another 2 to 3 pounds (.9 to 1.4 kg) for the head, legs, tail, and wings

Scales (optional)

Cutoff tool

Canvas work board

1/2-inch (1.3 cm) wooden slats

Rolling pin

5-inch (12.7 cm) round balloon

Pin tool

Ruler

Fork

Vinegar and water

Small sponge

Plastic card

Hair dryer

What To Do

1. Cut off 5 pounds (2.3 kg) of clay. It should be about the size of a cantaloupe.

2. Follow the directions for rolling out a slab on page 49. Use the ¹/₂-inch (1.3 cm) slats to get the right thickness.

3. Blow up the balloon, and tie it off. Don't blow it up too big, or it might pop. The balloon should be firm, but not stretched out all the way.

4. Use the pin tool to cut a strip off your slab that's 10 to 12 inches (25.4 to 30.5 cm) long and 4 to 5 inches (10.2 to 12.7 cm) wide. Set the balloon on the work board in front of you. Wrap the strip of slab around the bottom of the balloon. Score where the ends of the strip overlap, then dab on vinegar and water, and press them together well (see photo 1). The fork works well to score large areas like this, but be careful not to pop the balloon.

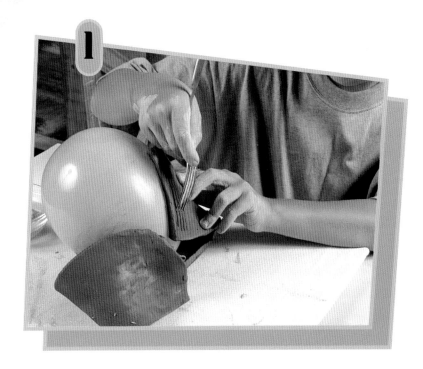

5. Cut another strip 3 to 4 inches (7.6 to 10.2 cm) wide and long enough to reach over the top of the balloon, and attach it to the bottom strip. Score and dab on vinegar and water where the ends meet. Keep cutting and adding strips like this, until the whole balloon is covered (except the very bottom, where it's sitting on the table), as shown in photo 2.

9. Now you can add the dragon's head, neck, feet, tail, wings, and any other features you like (see photo 4). Every dragon is different, so make it your way. Some dragons have horns, and some have large platelets that go down their back like a stegosaurus. Some dragons even have three heads! Just remember not to add any feature that's thicker than 1 inch (2.5 cm). If you're worried that a piece is too thick, hollow it out with your finger, then poke a hole with the pin tool to let steam escape when it's fired. If your dragon has a long tail, curl it back against the body—it's less likely to break off later.

Remember to always score, dab on vinegar and water, and seal anything you add. Have fun decorating your dragon!

6. Use the wooden slats to firmly tap the clay-covered balloon all over. This removes any air pockets that might have formed when the strips of clay were overlapped.

7. To get an even surface, smooth and scrape the clay all over with the plastic card (see photo 3).

8. Use the hair dryer for five minutes, until the clay is stiff but not completely dry.

10. When you're done adding dragon parts, push the pin tool through the clay to pop the balloon (see photo 5). Pull out the popped balloon through the bottom of the dragon. If you can't get it all out, just let it burn up in the kiln when the dragon is fired.

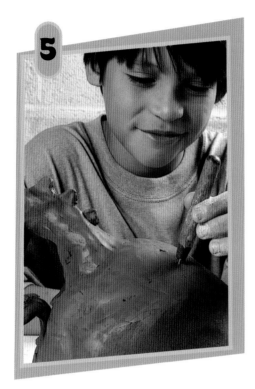

5

Dragons, Dragons, Everywhere

People all over the world have always had mythologies, or stories, about these magical creatures. In China, the dragon looked something like a snake with legs, and was thought to bring good luck. European dragons breathed fire and greedily guarded their treasures. In Ethiopia, dragons had four wings and they were big enough to kill elephants.

Where were all these dragons coming from? Scientists think that dragon myths started when people first discovered dinosaur bones. After all, if you were the first person to see a Tyrannosaurus Rex skeleton, what would you think?

Clay Clue

What if my balloon pops before I'm finished?

If the clay is stiff enough to hold its shape without the balloon, just keep working on it. If it's not, you'll have to blow up another balloon and start over.

I scraped a hole in the clay when I was smoothing it with the plastic card. Score carefully around the hole, then patch it by adding a small piece of slab. Smooth it in well with your fingers, then tap it firmly with a wooden slat to remove air pockets.

Bird Dome

A birdhouse doesn't have to be shaped square like a box—
or even made of wood at all. This birdhouse looks like a
dome tent. Little birds, like wrens and chickadees, will
think it's the perfect place to raise a family, and not nearly
as boring as a plain wooden box.

What You Need

7 pounds (3.2 kg) of clay
Scales (optional)
Cutoff tool
½-inch (1.3 cm) wooden slats
Rolling pin
Canvas work board
7-inch (17.8 cm) round balloon
Fork
Vinegar and water
Small sponge
Plastic card
Hair dryer
Pin tool
Ruler
¼-inch (6 mm) cord

What to Do

1. Cut off 7 pounds (3.2 kg) of clay. This much clay will be about the size of a honeydew melon.

2. Follow the directions on page 49 for rolling out a slab, using the ½-inch (1.3 cm) wooden slats.

3. Blow up the balloon until it's firm, but not over-stretched, and tie it off.

4. Tear or cut the slab into strips and overlap them, until the balloon is completely covered (see photo 1). Wherever the slab strips overlap, be sure to score the clay there with the fork, and dab on some vinegar and water. Be careful not to pop the balloon with the fork!

5. When the balloon is completely covered with clay, use one of the wooden slats to firmly tap it all over (see photo 2). This removes any air pockets that might have been trapped when you overlapped slab pieces.

6. Scrape and smooth the clay with the plastic card. Pick up the clay-covered balloon, and gently tap the bottom on the table to flatten it, so it won't roll away.

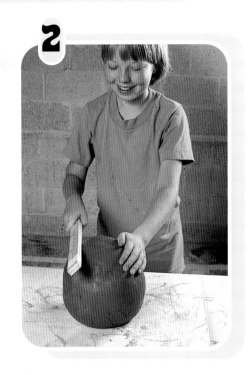

7. Use the hair dryer for five minutes, until the clay feels stiff but still bends when you press your finger against it.

8. Pinch off a small handful of clay, and roll out a coil $\frac{1}{2}$ inch (1.3 cm) thick and 2 to 3 inches (5 to 7.6 cm) long. Bend it into a circle, like a doughnut. Score the clay at the top of your round birdhouse, dab on some vinegar and water, and press the round coil in well. Be sure to seal the clay. This is where you'll tie the cord for hanging the birdhouse.

9. Now it's time to pop the balloon. Push the pin tool through the clay, until you hear the balloon pop. Because you used the hair dryer, the clay should be stiff enough to hold its shape.

10. With the ruler, measure 6 inches (15.2 cm) up from the bottom of the birdhouse, and make a mark there with the pin tool (see photo 3). This is where the birds like to have their entrance hole. Cut a round hole at the mark that is 1 $\frac{1}{2}$ inches (3.8 cm) across (see photo 4). Clay shrinks slightly when it's fired, so the hole will end up a little smaller than this. This is just the right size for wrens and chickadees.

11. Use the pin tool to make another small hole just underneath the entrance hole. After the birdhouse is fired, you can put a small twig there for a perch. Also make two or three small drainage holes in the bottom of the birdhouse, in case rainwater gets in.

12. If you can, shake the popped balloon out of the entrance. If not, just let it burn up in the kiln.

Talking Head

No, these heads can't really talk, but they look so realistic, they almost speak! You've probably drawn pictures of yourself or your friends, but have you ever made a life-size head in clay? Make a portrait head of someone you know well, like your best friend.

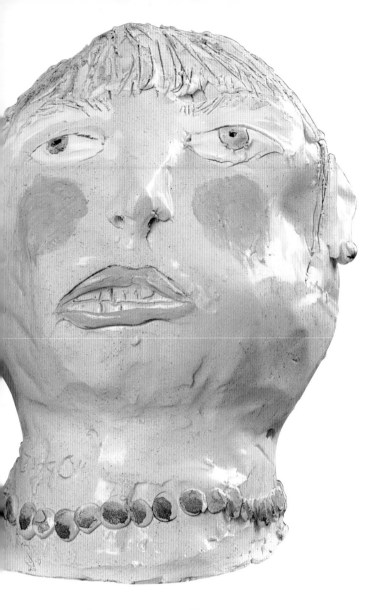

What You Need

5 pounds (2.3 kg) of clay for the head,
    3 pounds (1.4 kg) for the neck and
    shoulders, and a little more for the face
Cutoff tool
Scales (optional)
Canvas work board
Ruler
Pin tool
Fork
Vinegar and water
Small sponge
5-inch (12.7 cm) round balloon
Rolling pin
½-inch (1.3 cm) wooden slats
Plastic card
Hair dryer

card. Since the second coil is shorter than the first, it will make a circle that is a little smaller. This way the neck will be a little narrower than the shoulders. Having a wide base will also make it nice and steady when you add the head.

4. To make the neck higher, add one or two more coils the same thickness as the other coils. The shoulders and neck should be 4 to 5 inches (10.2 to 12.7 cm) high when you're done and a little wider at the bottom than the top.

What to Do

1. The first step is to build the neck and shoulders with three or four thick coils. For the first coil, start with 1 pound (.45 kg) of clay (about the size of an apple). Roll it out on the canvas work board into a coil, 8 to 10 inches (20.3 to 25.4 cm) long and 1 inch (2.5 cm) thick. If you have trouble rolling out such a long coil, roll out two shorter coils, then pinch the ends together to make a longer one.

2. Bend this coil into a circle, and pinch the ends together. Score all along the top of the coil with a pin tool or fork, and dab on vinegar and water.

3. Roll out another coil that is the same thickness but 2 or 3 inches (5.1 to 7.6 cm) shorter than the first coil. Press this one on top of the first coil you made (see photo 1). Smooth the seam together with your finger or a plastic

5. Now blow up the balloon, and tie it off. Place it on top of the neck so it fits inside it a little way (see photo 2).

6. Cut off another 5 pounds (2.3 kg) of clay, about the size of a cantaloupe.

7. Use the rolling pin and the ½-inch (1.3 cm) slats to flatten the clay into a slab (follow the instructions on page 49). This should be enough to cover the balloon. If not, you can always roll out a little more.

8. Use the pin tool to cut a strip from the slab that is 10 to 12 inches (25.4 to 30.5 cm) long and 3 to 4 inches (7.6 to 10.2 cm) wide. Wrap this around the bottom of the balloon so it overlaps the top of the neck a little. Score where the ends meet and where it overlaps. Dab on some vinegar and water, then smooth the seams with the plastic card.

9. Cut another strip the same size, and place it over the top of the balloon so the ends attach to the bottom strip you just put on. Score and seal the clay. Placing the strips this way keeps the balloon in place while you work.

10. Keep adding pieces of the slab until the whole balloon is covered. Score and seal the clay thoroughly wherever the slabs overlap.

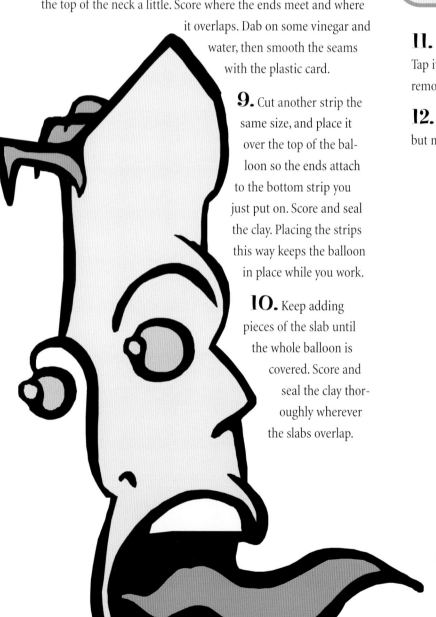

11. Scrape and smooth the clay with the plastic card. Tap it firmly all over with one of the wooden slats to remove air pockets.

12. Use the hair dryer for five minutes, until the clay is stiff but not completely dry.

13. Now you can add the nose, mouth, eyes, and hair (see photo 3). Be sure to score, dab on vinegar and water, and seal the clay each time you add a piece. Press all the features in well so they won't fall off as the clay dries. A wooden pencil works well for making nostrils or the pupils of the eyes. For hair, you could add flat strips or coils of clay, then scrape them with a fork for texture.

14. Every portrait is different, so it's up to you to make it look the way you want. When you're done, push the pin tool through the clay to pop the balloon. The popped balloon should drop through the bottom of the portait head. If you can't remove it all, don't worry. It will burn up in the kiln.

Powerful Portraits

Some of the world's most beautiful clay portrait heads were made in Africa over 2,000 years ago by a tribe of people called the Nok.

Not much is known about the Nok people, but when you look at their portrait heads, it's plain to see that they were superb artists. Each portrait has a unique expression. Most of the heads wear elaborately carved clay jewelry and have complex, braided hair styles. The Nigerian people of today, who are descended from the Nok, still wear their hair in the same beautiful hair styles as their ancestors.

Clay Clue

What should I do if a feature falls off while it's drying?

If the clay isn't completely dry, you can reattach it. Make a small batch of slurry (see page 19), then score and "glue" the part back on.

Slabs & Cylinders

So far, you've used slabs of clay to make curved and round forms. Now you'll get to use a cylinder, which is shaped like a hollow tube. You probably have a lot of cylinder shapes around your house, like iced tea glasses and soup cans. For these next six projects, you'll use a slab of clay to make some neat projects that start with a basic cylindrical shape. Check out the Glowing Lantern House on page 89—you'll be able to put a candle in it! And the awesomely huge Best Friends Totem Pole will look great in your room or backyard.

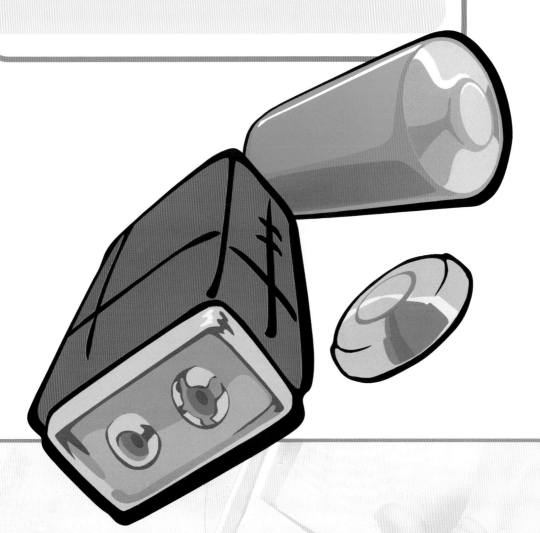

Skinny Nature Vase

You'll capture the outline of a flower, or maybe some pine needles, in this tall, skinny flower vase. All it takes is a cardboard tube, some clay, and a little piece of nature to imprint forever.

What You Need

3 to 4 pounds (1.4 to 1.8 kg) of clay

Scales (optional)

Cutoff tool

Canvas work board

Rolling pin

1/4-inch (6 mm) wooden slats

Pin tool

Ruler

Cardboard tube from a paper towel roll

Newspaper

Scissors

Tape

Hair dryer

Vinegar and water

Small sponge

Plant cuttings

What to Do

1. Start with 3 to 4 pounds (1.4 to 1.8 kg) of clay. You can weigh it out, or just guess. A 3-pound (1.4 kg) ball of clay is about the size of a grapefruit.

2. Roll out a slab of clay, using the 1/4-inch (6 mm) slats (see page 49 for more about rolling a slab).

3. With the pin tool and ruler, cut a strip that's 7 inches (17.8 cm) long and 6 to 8 inches (15.2 to 20.3 cm) wide. Let this strip lie flat on the table to dry a bit while you're working on getting the cardboard tube ready.

4. Cut or tear a piece of newspaper that's just big enough to cover the tube. Wrap it neatly around the tube, and secure it with a piece of tape (see photo 1). Be sure not to tape the newspaper directly to the tube. The tube should be able to slide freely inside the newspaper.

5. Go back to the strip of clay. Use the hair dryer for five minutes, to stiffen the clay a bit. You want the clay to hold its shape when you wrap it around the tube. If it's too soft, it will sag.

6. Set the tube on one end in front of you. Make sure the newspaper is even with the bottom of the tube. Wrap the strip of clay around the newspaper-covered tube (see photo 2). Score the clay where the ends overlap, dab on some vinegar and water, and press the ends together.

7. For the bottom, place the vase on an extra slab piece, and cut a circle around the vase with the pin tool. Score the edges of the circle, dab on vinegar and water, and press it into the vase. Be careful not to catch any newspaper between the clay pieces when you press them together. Smooth the seam with your fingers.

8. For the plant cutting, it's best to find a plant that's stiff and hard, like a holly leaf or pine needles. Soft flowers and plants don't make good impressions in the clay.

9. Press the cutting into the clay vase. Gently roll the vase on the work board until the plant is stuck in the clay (see photo 3). Pull the plant out of the clay, and you'll see the impression it left behind.

10. When your vase is done, it's time to remove the cardboard tube and newspaper. Pull the tube out first. The newspaper will keep it from sticking to the clay. Next, pull the newspaper out. If little pieces of newspaper stick inside the vase, don't try to remove them. They'll burn up in the kiln.

Clay Clue

What if some of the plant cuttings get stuck in the clay?

Don't worry if some of the plant stays stuck in the clay. It will burn up in the kiln.

Egyptian Canopic Jar

The Egyptians used ceremonial containers, called *canopic jars,* to hold the internal organs of important people who died. You can make a jar like the ancient ones did, but keep your special pens or your best marbles there instead. Use the Secret Cryptic Code to write your name on the jar in hieroglyphics.

What You Need

3 to 4 pounds (1.4 to 1.8 kg) of clay for
   the jar, and another 1 to 2 pounds
   (.45 to .9 kg) for the lid

Scales (optional)

Cutoff tool

Canvas work boad

½-inch (1.3 cm) wooden slats

Rolling pin

Pin tool

Ruler

Cardboard tube from paper towels

Newspaper

Scissors

Tape

Vinegar and water

Small sponge

Plastic card

Plastic wrap

What to Do

1. Start with 3 to 4 pounds (1.4 to 1.8 kg) of clay. A 3-
pound (1.4 kg) ball of clay is about the size of a grapefruit.

2. Use the rolling pin and the ½-inch (1.3 cm) slats to
roll the clay into a slab on the canvas work board (for
more about rolling slabs, see page 49).

3. With the pin tool and ruler, cut a rectangle from the
slab that's 6 inches (15.2 cm) wide and 7 inches (17.8
cm) long. Set it aside for the moment.

4. The cardboard tube from a paper towel roll will be a
little too long for this project. Use scissors to cut off 3
inches (7.6 cm) from one end (see photo 1). (Hint: You
might need a grownup to help.) Now you have a tube
that's 8 inches (20.3 cm) long.
Cut a piece of newspaper to fit the tube. Wrap it around
the tube and secure it with tape. Make sure the tube can
slide freely inside the newpaper (page 83 has a photo
showing the newspaper-wrapped tube).

5. Fit the 7-inch-long (17.8 cm) slab around the tube,
just as you did in the Skinny Nature Vase project. Score
the clay, dab on some vinegar and water, and seal it
where the slab overlaps.

6. For the bottom of the jar, place the clay tube upright
on an extra slab piece, and cut out a circle from around
the tube with the pin tool. Score the edges of the circle,
dab on vinegar and water, then press the bottom into the
jar. Seal the seam.

7. For the lid of your canopic jar, you'll make a pinch
pot and fit it, upside down, over the top of the jar. Start
with a ball of clay the size of an apple. Follow the pinch
pot directions in steps 3 through 5 for the Japanese Tea
Bowl on page 25.

8. Place the pinch pot upside down over the top of the
jar (see photo 2 on page 87). It should just fit over the
cardboard tube that's sticking out of the top. Score where

the pinch pot meets the clay jar, dab on some vinegar
and water, and seal the two pieces together. Use the plastic card to scrape and smooth the clay if it looks bumpy.
Now the cardboard tube is completely enclosed in clay.

You're probably wondering how you'll get the cardboard tube out. Don't worry, that's the last step.

9. The next step is to add features to the top of the jar, which you'll later turn into a lid (see photo 3). You can make your lid look like a falcon, baboon, jackal, or human, as the Egyptians did, or choose another animal. Each time you add a feature, such as an eye or an ear, be sure to score the clay and use some vinegar and water to help you seal it well.

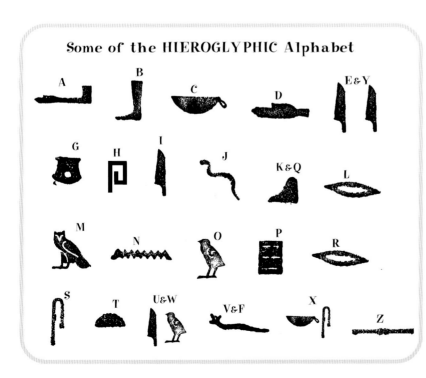

Some of the HIEROGLYPHIC Alphabet

A B C D E & Y

G H I J K & Q L

M N O P R

S T U & W V & F X Z

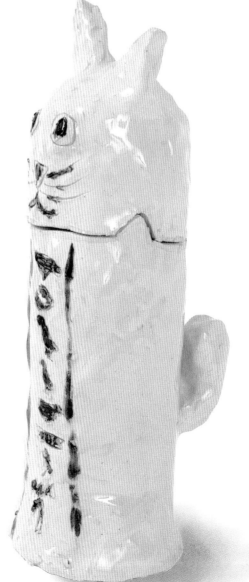

10. The Egyptians put hieroglyphics on the fronts of their jars. Use the Secret Cryptic Code to write your name on the jar, if you like. You can scratch the symbols in with the pin tool for now, and add glazes or underglazes later.

11. When you're done decorating your jar, it's time to cut off the lid. Choose a point near the top, where you added the pinch pot, and push the pin tool into the side of the jar. Carefully cut all the way around the jar with the pin tool. Make your cut wavy, instead of straight (see photo 4), to help the lid lock in place. The lid could easily fall off if you used a straight cut.

12. Remove the lid, and carefully set it aside. Now you can pull out first the cardboard tube, then the newspaper.

13. Put a piece of plastic wrap over the top of the jar, then carefully put the lid back on. The plastic will keep the lid from sticking to the jar while it dries.

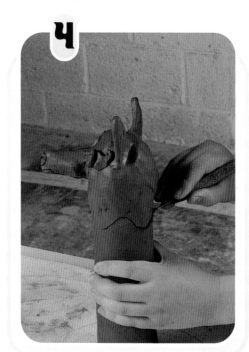

I Want My Mummy!

Removing the internal organs from a dead body was part of the mummification process used by the ancient Egyptians for thousands of years. Each organ went into a particular canopic jar for safe-keeping. The lids of the jars were decorated with the four sons of the god Horus. The first son, Imsety, the human, protected the liver. Qebekh-sennuef, the falcon, guarded the intestines. Hapy, the baboon, looked over the lungs. Duamutef, the jackal, kept the stomach.

The heart was considered the very center of the person's being, and was not removed. The brain, on the other hand, was sucked out the nose and discarded! So much for brainpower!

Clay Clue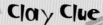

What if the newspaper sticks inside my jar? Wait until the jar dries some more, then you can pull on the newspaper a little harder. If it still sticks to the clay, don't worry. It will burn up in the kiln.

Glowing Lantern House

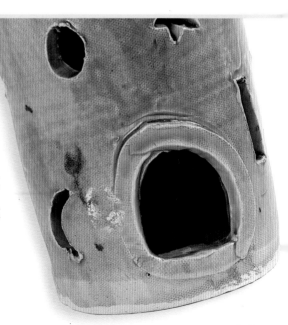

Light up your backyard for summer night cookouts or backyard camping with this neat fireproof lantern. The cutouts will make great shadow-shapes!

What You Need

5 pounds (2.3 kg) of clay for the lantern
  walls, and another 2 to 3 pounds
  (.9 to 1.4 kg) for the lid

Scales (optional)

Cutoff tool

Canvas work board

Rolling pin

1/2-inch (1.3 cm) wooden slats

Ruler

Pin tool

Newspaper

Scissors

Tape

#10 can

Vinegar and water

Small sponge

Plastic card

Disposable plastic salad bowl

Plastic wrap

What to Do

1. Cut off 5 pounds (2.3 kg) of clay, and roll it into a slab, using the 1/2-inch (1.3 cm) slats (read more about rolling slabs on page 49). This much clay would be about the size of a cantaloupe if you rolled it into a ball.

2. Use the ruler and pin tool to cut a rectangle 15 inches (38.1 cm) long and 7 inches (17.8 cm) wide.

3. Cover the #10 can with a sheet of newspaper, and secure it with a piece of tape. Make sure the can slides freely inside the newspaper.

4. To make the lantern house walls, wrap the slab rectangle around the newspaper-covered can. Score the clay where it overlaps, then dab on some vinegar and water, and press it together. Smooth the seam with your finger or a plastic card.

5. Use the pin tool to cut shapes in the walls of your lantern (see photo 1). You can cut stars, circles, triangles, ovals, or any other shape you like. Try patterns like tree leaves, or make a shape like the sun or the moon. Just be careful not to cut too many shapes that are too close together, and none of the cutouts should be too big. That would weaken the walls. Keep the shapes 2 to 3 inches (5 to 7.6 cm) apart.

6. When you're done, pull the can out of the lantern, then pull out the newspaper.

7. For the lid, cut off another 2 to 3 pounds (.9 to 1.4 kg) of clay, and roll it into a slab on the canvas work board. Cover the outside of the salad bowl with plastic wrap, then drape the slab over the bowl. Trim off the edges with the pin tool so that you have a round lid the size and shape of the bowl (see photo 2).

8. Cut out two or three small shapes in the lid. The smoke from the candle will escape through these holes. To make a handle for the top of the lid, cut a small strip from an extra slab piece, and bend it into a U shape. To attach the handle to the lid, score the clay on the lid and the handle ends. Use a bit of vinegar and water, then press the handle in well (see photo 3).

9. Drape some plastic wrap over the top of the lantern, then put on the lid. The plastic will keep the lid from sticking while it dries. After the lantern is glazed and fired, put a candle inside for a cool nighttime lamp.

Hollow Stump Planter

Clay is the perfect material to pick up different textures. You can make clay look like cloth, leather, or smooth metal—almost any kind of surface. Take a close look at the bark on a tree, then make the clay look like bark for this hollow stump planter. Then, for fun, put it in the garden!

What You Need

5 pounds (2.3 kg) of clay for the outside of the stump and another 2 to 3 pounds (.9 to 1.4 kg) for the bottom of the stump

Scales (optional)

Cutoff tool

Rolling pin

Canvas work board

1/2-inch (1.3 cm) wooden slats

Ruler

Scissors

Newspaper

Tape

Large, empty tin can

Pin tool

Vinegar and water

Small sponge

Fork

Bark samples from trees

Pictures of trees and stumps

What to Do

1. Start with 5 pounds (2.3 kg) of clay. Rolled into a ball, this much clay should be the size of a cantaloupe. Follow the directions for rolling out a slab, using the 1/2-inch (1.3 cm) slats.

2. Cut or tear a strip from your slab that is 15 inches (38.1 cm) long and 6 to 8 inches (15.2 to 20.3 cm) wide. You don't need to cut straight lines. The stump will look more natural with uneven, jagged edges.

3. Cut a sheet of newspaper so that it will just fit around the #10 can. The newspaper should be even with the bottom of the can. It's okay if it's longer at the top. Secure the newspaper with a piece of tape. Be careful not to tape the newspaper directly to the can. The can should be able to slide freely inside the newspaper.

4. Wrap the strip of clay around the can. Score the clay, dab on vinegar and water, and seal it where the ends overlap (see photo 1).

5. Look closely at your pictures of trees. See how the roots form little humps at the bottom of the tree? Add slab scraps at the bottom of the stump to look like roots. You can also make knotholes or add mushrooms and lichens—even tiny insects!—to your stump (see photo 2). For bark texture, scrape the fork through the clay. Try a lot of different techniques to get what you want.

6. For the bottom of the stump, roll out another slab, using 2 to 3 pounds (.9 to 1.4 kg) of clay. With the can still inside, put the stump on top of the slab. Trace around the stump to get the correct shape for the bottom, then cut it out with the pin tool. Score the edges, use a little vinegar and water on the scoring, then press the bottom in well. Use your finger to seal the seam all the way around.

7. The last step is to remove the can. This is important. Clay shrinks a little as it dries. If you leave the can in, the clay will crack as it dries because it can't shrink enough around with the can in the way.

8. Pull out the can first, then peel out the newspaper. Any small pieces of paper left in the clay will burn up safely in the kiln.

Beautiful Bumpily Bark

Take a walk in the woods and notice the bark on the trees. Does all bark look the same? Hardly! Some bark is smooth, some scaly. Other bark might have ridges, or look cracked and flaky. Different kinds of trees have different kinds of bark. Bark from a birch tree is paper thin, but bark from a giant sequoia can be two feet (.6 m) thick.

Bark is like the tree's skin. It protects the inner core of the tree from injuries, water loss, diseases, or animal pests. So don't be a pest yourself; if you want a bark sample, peel it off a dead, fallen tree, not a live one. You wouldn't want someone peeling off your skin!

Best Friends Totem Pole

Fierce ravens, bears, and wolves here tell a mythical tale. Grab your friends and tell a story with your own clay totem pole. It's a lot quicker than carving one!

What You Need

3 or 4 large, empty tin cans

Newspaper

Scissors

Tape

5 pounds (2.3 kg) of clay for each section
of the totem pole

Cutoff tool

Rolling pin

½-inch (1.3 cm) wooden slats

Canvas work board

Ruler

Pin tool

Vinegar and water

Small sponge

Pictures of Northwest Indian
totem poles

3-inch (7.6 cm) piece of PVC pipe
or a 2 x 4 (3.8 x 8.9 cm) wooden board

What to Do

1. To make one segment of the totem pole, you'll need one coffee can. Cut or fold several sheets of newspaper so they're the same height as the coffee can. Cover the can with the paper, and secure it with tape.

2. Cut off 5 pounds (2.3 kg) of clay, about the size of a cantaloupe. Use the rolling pin and the wooden slats to roll out a slab on the canvas work board.

3. Use the ruler and pin tool to cut a rectangle from the slab that's 6 x 15 inches (15.2 x 38.1 cm). Wrap the clay rectangle around the can. Score with the pin tool where the ends overlap. Dab on vinegar and water, and seal the seam (see photo 1). Make sure the top of the clay is even with the can. If the clay is uneven at the top, the segments of the totem pole won't stack evenly when you're done.

4. Now you're ready to add the face. Look at pictures of totem poles to get ideas. The Northwest Indians often depict bears, ravens, eagles, and orcas. Human and animal forms usually look very fierce, with lots of teeth and claws. See if you can create an animal or human in the same style.

5. When you're done, pull out the can and newspaper, and let this segment of the totem pole dry. Make as many segments as you want. When they're glazed and fired, stack them together over a pipe or wooden board. PVC pipe comes in many different widths. You can get it cut to any length you want at a hardware store. To stabilize the pole, bury the bottom of the pipe or board partway in the ground. If you want your totem pole inside, you might need to attach the pole to a wooden base. Get a grownup to help. Photo 2 shows how the totem parts stack together.

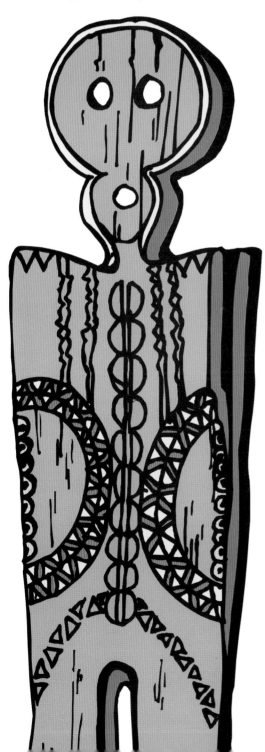

Friends, Family, and Totem Poles

Totem poles were carved by Native American tribes in the Pacific Northwest to put in front of their homes and lodges. The fantastic creatures carved into these wooden poles told about important events and legends in the families' history—kind of like the family crest. Totem poles were erected as part of an important ceremony called the potlatch. In a long ago potlatch ceremony, a family showed its generosity by throwing a big "giveaway" party, where they gave away almost everything they owned, even names and dances. By the end of the potlatch party, the family might not have a pot left to cook in, but they would have lots and lots of friends!

Haniwa

Hani....what? Not many people know what a haniwa is. Haniwa sculptures look like people. They're fun to look at because even though they're very simple, they show a lot of different expressions. You can give your haniwa a certain expression, just as Japanese sculptors did long ago. Then put your new friend in your room or in the family garden.

What You Need

2 large, empty tin cans

Can opener

Newspaper

Scissors

Tape

7 pounds (3.2 kg) of clay for the cylinder
  body, 3 pounds (1.4 kg) for the head,
  and 2 pounds (.9 kg) for the arms

Cutoff tool

Rolling pin

Canvas work board

1/2-inch (1.3 cm) wooden slats

Ruler

Pin tool

Vinegar and water

Small sponge

Plastic card

Balloon

Hair dryer

What to Do

1. Use the can opener to remove the bottoms from the
two coffee cans. (It will be easier to pull the cans out of
your haniwa when you're done if the bottoms are gone.)
Run them through the can opener several times, until
all the sharp edges are gone. Stack the cans, one on top
of the other. Wrap three or four sheets of newspaper
around the cans, and secure the sheets with tape (see
photo 1). Fold or cut the newspaper so that it's the same
height as the cans.

2. Cut off 7 pounds (3.2 kg) of clay. It will be the size of
a large cantaloupe. Drop it hard on the canvas work
board a few times to start flattening it. Use the rolling
pin and the 1/2-inch (1.3 cm) wooden slats to roll out a
slab. Use the pin tool and ruler to cut out a rectangle
from the slab that's 12 inches (30.5 cm) by 15 inches
(38.1 cm).

3. Wrap the slab around the cans. With the pin tool,
score the clay where the ends overlap (see photo 2), and
dab on vinegar and water. Smooth and seal the seam
with the plastic card.

4. Blow up the balloon, tie it off, then place it on the
top coffee can so that it fits partway inside.

5. Cut off another 3 pounds (1.4 kg) of clay. Roll it into a slab that's 7 to 8 inches (17.8 to 20.3 cm) long. Use the pin tool to cut wide strips from the slab. Fit the strips over the top of the balloon (see photo 3). Score the ends of the strips where they meet with the clay cylinder. Smooth all the seams carefully with the plastic card. Keep working until the balloon is covered. This will be the haniwa's head. Tap it firmly with one of the wooden slats to remove any air pockets.

6. Use the hair dryer on the head for five minutes or so, until the clay is slightly stiff.

7. Use the pin tool to cut out shapes from your extra slab pieces for the ears and nose. To attach them, score the clay, and dab on vinegar and water. You can also use slab pieces to make a belt or skirt, if you want. Cut holes in the head for the eyes and mouth (see photo 4). Experiment with different shapes to get the expression you want. You may want to sketch some different expressions on a piece of paper before you cut into the clay. The balloon will probably pop when you cut out the eyes or mouth. That's okay, since the clay is slightly stiff now. It will hold its shape.

8. To make the arms, roll out two coils that are 1 inch (2.5 cm) thick and 8 to 10 inches (20.3to 25.4cm) long. Score one end of each coil, dab on vinegar and water, then press them in firmly. Position them however you like (just remember that the arms might get broken off if they stick straight out).

9. Let the project sit for an hour or two when you're done so the clay can stiffen a little more. Then get someone to help you lift it while you remove the cans from the inside of the haniwa. Wrap the haniwa in plastic, and let it dry slowly for several days.

Clay Clue

How can I tell when my haniwa is really dry?

Bone dry clay is powdery looking. If you're not sure, touch it gently and it will feel like dry chalk.

Gentle Guardians

Haniwa sculptures were made in Japan thousands of years ago, to guard the burial mounds of important leaders. Lots of these clay guardians were needed for every burial mound, so sculptors learned to make them very quickly and simply from large, hollow clay cylinders. The word *haniwa* means "circle of clay."

Instead of giving each haniwa guard the fierce expression of a warrior, most of them have gentle, happy, or sometimes silly looks on their faces. Haniwas are much loved in Japan today because of their humanness and gentle sense of humor.

Slab Constructions

Now that you know some of the fun things you can do with slabs, you can try some unusual slab projects. It's a challenge to put them together because they have more parts. Some of the parts need to be just the right size if you're going to get a real-looking wizard or a puzzle-top box.

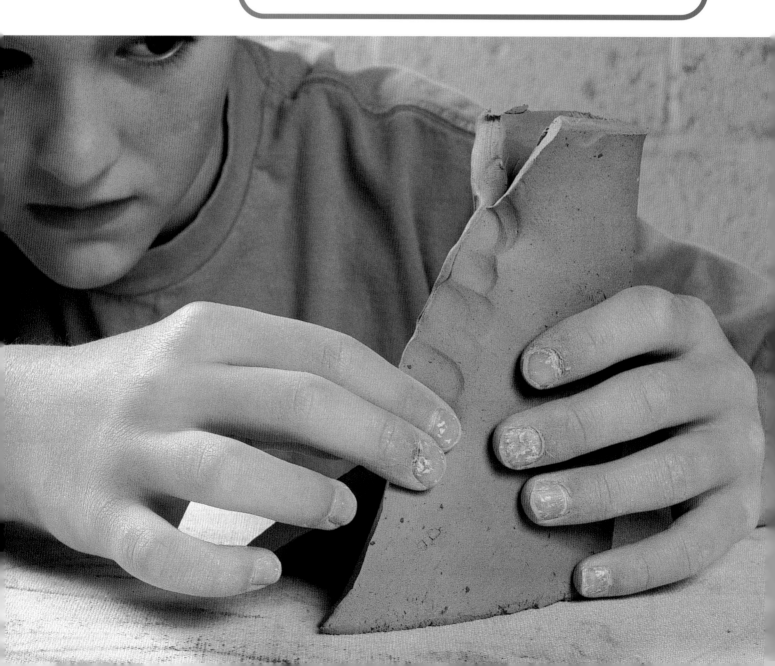

Puzzle-Top Box

It's not such a big mystery after all. To keep the lid from sliding off, you'll cut it so that it fits the bottom of the box like a puzzle piece.

What to Do

1. Start with 5 pounds (2.3 kg) of clay (this much clay is about the size of a cantaloupe). With the rolling pin, roll the clay into a slab on the canvas work board, using the ½-inch (1.3 cm) slats. Page 49 shows how to roll out a slab.

2. Open up the top of the empty milk carton, then spread it out flat. You'll see that it's made up of four rectangles, each measuring 3 x 4 inches (7.6 x 10.2 cm). Cut out one of the rectangles with your scissors. This will be the template.

3. Place the template on the slab of clay. Use the pin tool to carefully cut around the template, making a clay rectangle the same size (see photo 1). Do this three more times, so that you have four clay rectangles the same size. Cut the rectangles as close together as possible, so you'll have some extra slab left over. Save the extra. You'll need it later.

What You Need

5 pounds (2.3 kg) of clay
Cutoff tool
Scales (optional)
Canvas work board
½-inch (1.3 cm) wooden slats
Rolling pin
Empty half-pint (.24 L) milk carton
Scissors
Pin tool
Hair dryer
Rubber stamps (optional)
Vinegar and water
Small sponge
Wooden craft stick

4. To stiffen them a bit, use the hair dryer for five minutes on each of the clay rectangles. Make sure they're lying flat as you dry them. You want the clay rectangles to be just stiff enough to hold their shape without sagging when you begin to assemble the box. If you want, press a rubber stamp into the rectangles for decoration (see photo 2).

5. Before you start putting the box together, score all of the edges of one of the rectangles with the pin tool. Dampen the places you scored with vinegar and water.

6. Stand the scored rectangle on one end, then press another rectangle into the scored edge, so they fit together like the sides of a box. Press another rectangle onto the other scored edge of the first rectangle (see photo 3). Now you have three sides of a box.

7. Score all of the edges of the last rectangle, and dab vinegar and water onto the scoring. Press this rectangle into place, so that your box has four sides. Putting the box together in this order will keep the sides from getting crooked.

8. To make the bottom, place the box on an extra slab piece. Use the pin tool to trace, then cut, a square piece of clay to fit the bottom (see photo 4). Score the edges of the bottom piece, dab on some vinegar and water, then press the bottom piece on.

9. Use the wooden craft stick to carefully smooth together all the seams where the sides meet. For extra strength, you can roll out tiny coils about the size of earthworms, and press these into the inside seams of the box. Smooth out the coils with the wooden craft stick.

10. Now you're ready to add the top. Turn the box upside down on an extra slab piece. Use the pin tool to trace around the edges, then cut out a square, just as you did for the bottom piece. Score the clay square, dab on vinegar and water, and press the top in place. Smooth the seams with the craft stick.

11. Your box is now completely enclosed. To make the puzzle-top lid, push the pin tool through the side of the box, near the top, and cut a wavy line all the way around. You can remove the lid now, then put it back on the box. Notice that it only fits one way.

12. Because of all the seams, it's important that the box dries slowly and evenly. If it dries too fast, you could get cracks where the sides meet. Wrap the box loosely in plastic wrap, and set it aside for a few days. Then remove the plastic wrap, and let it finish drying completely.

Clay Clue

What if I get cracks as my box dries?

If you get cracks, you can sometimes repair them by rubbing a little clay mixed with vinegar and water into the cracks.

Egyptian Pyramid

No need to ride a camel to Egypt! Instead, you can harness the power
of the pyramids at home. If you can make a box, you can make a
pyramid—a small one, that is! When you're done, decorate it with
hieroglyphics (look on page 87 for the Secret Cryptic Code).

What You Need

1 sheet of construction or other stiff paper
Scissors
Pencil
Ruler
6 pounds (2.7 kg) of clay
Cutoff tool
Canvas work board
Rolling pin
½-inch (1.3 cm) wooden slats
Pin tool
Hair dryer
Vinegar and water
Small sponge
Plastic card

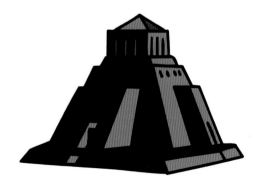

What to Do

1. To make a pyramid, you'll need a template shaped like a triangle and one shaped like a square. On some construction paper (or any stiff paper), use a ruler and pencil to draw a triangle that is 6 inches (15.2 cm) long on each side. Cut out the triangle with the scissors. Now draw a square that is 6 inches (15.2 cm) on all sides, and cut it out with scissors. These will be your templates.

2. Cut off 5 pounds (2.3 kg) of clay. This much clay will be about the size of a cantaloupe. Use the rolling pin and the ½-inch (1.3 cm) slats to roll it into a slab on the canvas work board.

3. Place the triangular template on the slab of clay. Use the pin tool to cut out four triangles from the slab, tracing around the template four different times (see photo 1). Place the square template on the slab, and cut out one square. Lay the four triangles and the square flat on the work board, and dry them for five minutes each with the hair dryer. The clay pieces should be fairly stiff when you're done, but not completely dry.

4. Use the pin tool to score all along the edges of the square. Now score the edge of one side of one triangle. Dab on vinegar and water where you scored the clay. Pick up this

triangle and another triangle. Place the two triangles along two sides of the square where you scored the clay. Fit the edges of the two triangles together at the scoring (see photo 2). Smooth the seams carefully with the plastic card. Once they're connected, the two triangles should stand up on their own.

5. Score the third triangle along all the edges. Dab on vinegar and water. Press this triangle against the edge of the second triangle so you have three of the sides fitted together on top of the square bottom. Smooth the seams together with the plastic card.

6. Score the edges of the fourth triangle, dab on some vinegar and water, and press it into place. Now you have a four-sided pyramid like the ones the Egyptians made. Smooth all the seams with the plastic card (see photo 3).

7. To be able to put things inside your pyramid, make a lid by cutting the top off with the pin tool (see photo 4). Make an uneven cut like you did for the Puzzle-Top Box (see the photo on page 103). That way, the lid will stay in place and not fall off easily.

8. If you want your pyramid to be simply decorative, don't cut a lid off the top. Instead, make a small hole with the pin tool near the top of the pyramid so that hot air can escape when it's fired.

9. The pyramid must dry slowly and evenly, so cover your pyramid loosely with plastic wrap.

Clay Clue

What if my pyramid's sides don't fit together right?

Be sure to cut all the triangle shapes exactly the same size.

Really Big Building Project

The pyramids were invented by the Egyptians over 4,000 years ago to serve as tombs for the pharaohs. These immense structures were built from solid stone blocks, weighing up to 5 tons (4.5 t) each. The Great Pyramid, one of the oldest structures on the face of the earth, has a base that covers 13 acres (5.2 ha). It's one of the few man-made structures large enough to be seen from outer space!

The most amazing fact of all about the pyramids is that they were built without the aid of the wheel, or even any kind of special tools. Archeologists have many different theories about how those great stone blocks were put into place. Most agree that it must have taken lots and lots and lots of manpower. A small clue to the mystery is carved into the side of one of the giant stone blocks that makes up the Great Pyramid. It's a hieroglyphic message that reads "this end up."

Mystical Wizard

Let your imagination go back to the mysterious time of wizards, magic, and sorcery. Put on your long cloak and pointed wizard hat, then make a little magic yourself by turning a piece of clay into a wizard!

What You Need

2 pounds (.9 kg) of clay
Cutoff tool
Rolling pin
Canvas work board
¼-inch (6 mm) wooden slats
Pin tool
Ruler
Newspaper
Vinegar and water
Small sponge

What to Do

1. Use the cutoff tool to slice off 2 pounds (.9 kg) of clay. It should be about the size of a large orange.

2. Roll all of the clay out on the canvas work board. Use the slats to get the right thickness. If you've been using two yardsticks put together as your slats, take them apart. One yardstick is ¼ inch (6 mm) thick.

3. Use your pin tool and ruler to cut a triangle that is 7 inches (17.8 cm) on all three sides. You can make it a little bigger or a little smaller if you want. Save all the slab scraps after you cut the big triangle. You'll need them later.

4. Measure down 2 inches (5 cm) from the top of the triangle. Use the pin tool to cut off the top 2 inches (5 cm) of the triangle (see photo 1). Save the top triangle piece. You'll need it later to make the wizard's hat.

5. Pick up the big triangle, which no longer has a top. Bend the sides toward each other, and pinch them together to make an ice cream cone shape (see photo 2). Leave the narrow end of the cone open. This is where the head fits in later.

6. Set the cone shape on your work board, with the wide end of the cone at the bottom. Tear off a piece of newspaper, crumple it, and stuff it inside the cone. This helps support the clay cone so it can stand on its own.

7. To make the collar at the top of the cloak, pinch the clay at the top of the cone (where you left it open), and gently fold it down. The head will fit inside here.

8. Make sleeves with the extra slab pieces. Use the pin tool to cut two small triangles that are 2 inches (5 cm) on each side. Fold these two triangles into cone shapes. Pinch the sides together where they meet.

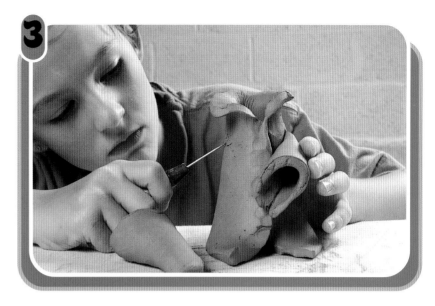

9. Use the pin tool to score the clay near the top of the cloak, where you want to attach the sleeves (see photo 3). Dab on a little vinegar and water where you scored. Press the narrow end of the cone-shaped sleeves into the scored part. Seal them well. The sleeves will be wider at the bottom than at the top. Bend them so they fit closely against the cloak. If you leave them sticking straight out, they might break off later.

11. Push the neck into the opening at the top of the cloak. Squeeze the cloak tightly shut around the neck, to keep the head from rolling off (see photo 4).

10. Now you have an invisible wizard! To make him visible, let's first add a head. Pinch off a piece of clay about the size of a large grape. Roll it into a ball. Gently pinch and pull a neck out from the ball.

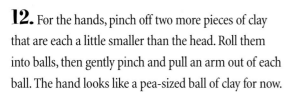

12. For the hands, pinch off two more pieces of clay that are each a little smaller than the head. Roll them into balls, then gently pinch and pull an arm out of each ball. The hand looks like a pea-sized ball of clay for now.

13. Push the arm up the sleeve, then squeeze the sleeve around it so it doesn't fall out. To make fingers, partly slice the ball in three or four places with the pin tool.

14. Now go back to the head. Remember when you cut the top 2 inches (5 cm) off the big triangle? You'll make a wizard's hat out of it. Fold the sides of this small triangle piece together to make an ice cream cone shape. Pinch the sides together well.

15. Score the top of the wizard's head, dab on a little vinegar and water, then place the hat on his head. If it's too small, gently stretch it out a little with your fingers. Firmly press the hat onto his head.

16. Now you can give your wizard a face. First, use your fingers to pinch out a little clay from the face, to make a nose. Use your pin tool to make two little holes for nostrils.
Score where you want to add eyes. To make eyeballs, roll tiny balls of clay with your fingers. Firmly press them in where you scored. Draw in the iris and pupil of each eye with a pin tool.

17. To make a long, flowing beard, first score a place under the nose where you want the beard, then dab on a little vinegar and water. Flatten a little strip of clay for the beard, and press it in where you scored (see photo 5). Use the pin tool to scratch hair texture.

18. Your wizard is now complete, except for any small details you'd like to add. Draw a moon or stars on his hat with the pin tool. Or you might want to position his hand so he can hold a marble (for a crystal ball) after he's been glazed and fired.

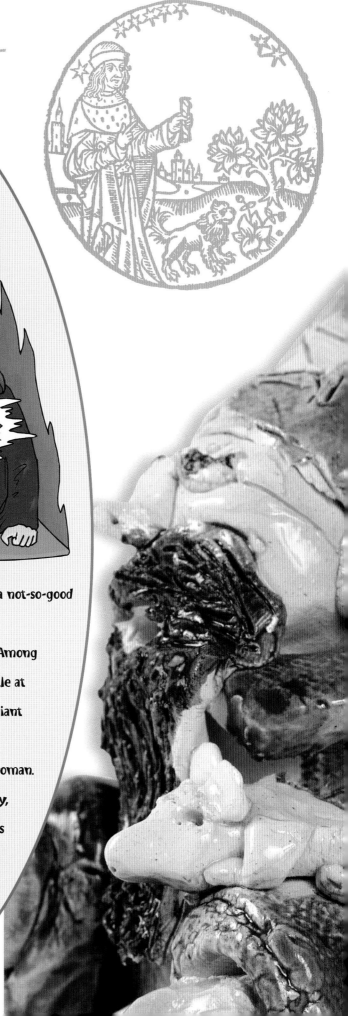

What A Wizard!

Merlin was a very famous wizard in the long ago times of King Arthur. According to legend, when Arthur was made king, Merlin became his advisor. Merlin could change himself into the shape of any animal. When King Arthur needed a message delivered quickly, Merlin changed into a stag and swiftly ran with it.

Merlin had many magic objects, including a cup that told whether the drinker had led a good, pure life. The cup always overflowed when it touched the lips of a not-so-good person.

Merlin is said to have performed many great feats of magic. Among these were the magical creation of the Round Table and the castle at Camelot. Some legends say that he also magically erected the giant stones at Stonehenge.

Merlin's one flaw was that he liked the wrong kind of woman. Viviane, the Lady of the Lake, enticed him with her beauty, then learned all of his magical secrets. Once she knew his magic, Viviane imprisoned Merlin in an underground palace. There he remains, forever unchanged by time, and always increasing his store of knowledge.

Glazing and Firing

Decorating your clay projects with colors is the final step in the ceramic process. Adding color to any artwork can be fun and exciting. With pottery, it's even more exciting because the glaze colors you use will turn to glass when the piece is fired again. Glazes not only beautify your projects, they also protect them with a hard, glossy, waterproof coating.

What Are Glazes?

Glazes are a mixture of ground glass (silica) and different kinds of colorants mixed in water. The glazes you'll use come in jars, with each color written on the label. Don't be surprised, though, if the label says the glaze is "yellow," but it looks brown when you open the jar. Quite often, a glaze is a different color before it's fired.

Paint glaze on your project with a paintbrush or, if you have enough glaze, dip your project into a bucket of glaze. Before you begin glazing, there are some important rules to remember. Be sure to read each rule carefully.

Rules for Glazing

1. Glazes are only for bisque-fired ceramic pieces. Putting a glaze on greenware can result in damage to the kiln or to your project.

2. Only use glazes marked non-toxic and lead free.

3. Potters use a special kind of liquid wax, called wax resist, to keep glaze off the bottom of their pots. Supply stores that sell glazes also carry wax resist. Paint a little of the resist on the bottom (and the lid, if you have one) of your bisque-fired project before you glaze it.

Wax is very runny, so it's best to paint it on with the project on its side. If you turn the piece upside down, the wax could run down the sides. Wax is made to keep glaze off, so wherever you paint wax, you won't be able to paint glaze.

For more about glazing lidded projects, see the instructions for Glazing a Lidded Project on page 117.

4. Always wipe any glaze off the bottom of your projects before they're put in the kiln for the glaze firing.

Glazes melt and turn to glass when they're heated in the kiln. If you leave glaze on the bottom of your piece, the glaze will harden and stick the project to the kiln shelf. Glaze will bead up over the wax resist, so be sure to wipe that part clean.

5. Wash your hands thoroughly after glazing. Wear a smock to keep glaze off your clothes.

6. Keep food and drinks away from your glazing area.

Glazing a Lidded Project

A project with a lid needs special attention when you glaze it to make sure the lid doesn't stick during the firing. Here's how to properly apply wax resist, then glaze, to a puzzle-top box.

What You Need

Bisque-fired puzzle-top box
Newspaper
Jar of wax resist, 2 ounces (60 mL)
Paintbrushes, ½ to 1 inch (1.3 to 2.5 cm) wide
Water, to rinse brushes
Low-fire, nontoxic glazes, in any color
Small sponge

What to Do

1. To keep it clean, spread some newspaper on your worktable. Take the lid off the box, then place the box on its side in front of you.

2. Open the jar of wax resist. With the brush, paint a thin, even coat of wax on the bottom of your box (see photo 1). Paint a ¼-inch (6 mm) strip of wax along the bottom edge, so that the glaze won't run down during the firing. Wax is very runny, so it's best to paint it on with the box on its side. If you turn the box upside down, the wax could run down the sides. Wax is made to keep glaze off, so wherever you paint wax, you can't paint glaze.

3. Now paint a thin layer of wax on the top edge of your box. Paint another thin layer along the "puzzle" edge of the lid (see photo 2). Keep the box and the lid on their sides while you work, so that the wax won't run down the sides.

4. The wax dries in about five minutes. While you're waiting, rinse your brush thoroughly in water.

5. Now it's time to apply the glaze. Before you open it, shake the jar vigorously—make sure the lid is tightly screwed on! Open the jar, and use your clean brush to paint the glaze on the box and lid. Don't forget to paint the inside as well as the outside of the pieces. Paint two or three coats on, so the color will be smooth, not streaky. You can use more than one color for your design or, for an interesting effect, paint one color over another. Some other fancy glaze effects to try:

 *Dab glaze on with a sponge
 *Drip one glaze over another
 *Splatter (carefully!) glaze with the brush

6. When you're done, and the glaze is dry, use a damp sponge to wipe off any glaze that beaded up over the wax resist (see photo 3). It should be quick and easy to remove. Place the lid back on the box. Now it's ready for the kiln.

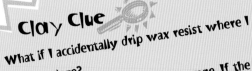

Dipping with Tongs

A quick way to get a nice, even coat of glaze on your projects is to use a pair of tongs to dip them into a bucket of glaze. The tongs keep you from having to put your hands in the glaze. You can buy dipping tongs at a ceramic supply shop. Remember, only dip projects that have been bisque fired, and always put on wax resist first. Never put glaze on an unfired piece. You can dip your bisque-fired projects in any color glaze. Or, if you've used underglazes, you can dip the piece in a clear glaze, so that the underglaze designs show through. Most supply shops sell low-fire glazes in powdered form. You mix the powder with water right in the bucket.

What You Need

Disposable rubber gloves

Dust mask

Powdered low-fire glaze,
   3 pounds (1.4 kg)

1-gallon (3.8 L) bucket

Wooden paint stirrer

Water

Newspaper to spread over the
   work area

Bisque-fired project

Wax resist

Small paintbrush

Dipping tongs

Small sponge

Clay Clue

What if I accidentally drip wax resist where I want to put glaze?
Wipe it off immediately with a damp sponge. If the wax is still there, use sandpaper to lightly sand it off.

What if I painted glaze on the bottom of my project where wax resist should be instead?
Wipe or scrub off the glaze with a damp sponge, then paint on the wax resist where it should go. Reapply glaze in bare spots if you need to.

What to Do

1. Mixing glazes can be messy. Put on a pair of disposable rubber gloves and a dust mask so you won't breathe in any of the dry glaze powder. Put the dry glaze in the bucket, and add 3 to 4 quarts (2.8 to 3.8 L) of water.

2. Stir the mixture thoroughly with the wooden paint stirrer. When you're done, the mixture should look like heavy cream (see photo 1).

3. Spread some newspaper over your work area. Using a small brush, paint a thin layer of wax resist on the bottom of your bisque-fired piece. Also paint a 1/4-inch (6 mm) strip of wax along the bottom edge of the project. If the piece has a lid, paint some wax there, too (see page 117 for more about glazing lidded projects). Let the wax dry for three to five minutes. Rinse the brush in water.

4. Pick up the project carefully with the tongs, and dip it into the glaze mixture. Make sure the mixture gets on the inside of the project, too. Count to three, then pull the piece out, making sure to turn it so that any glaze on the inside pours out into the bucket (see photo 2).

5. Set the project on the newspaper to dry. It shouldn't take more than five minutes.

6. When the glaze is dry, pick up the project and use a damp sponge to quickly wipe off any glaze that may have beaded up over the waxed areas.

Clay Clue

What if my project is too big to fit in the bucket? For large projects, place wooden slats over the top of the bucket, then carefully balance the project on top of the slats. Dip out some glaze with a plastic cup, then pour it over the project, so that the glaze runs back into the bucket (see photo 3). Keep pouring, until you cover the whole project. Wear disposable rubber gloves to keep the glaze off your hands.

Underglazes

Underglazes are colors you can paint on your projects. They're designed to go under a coat of clear, transparent glaze. Underglazes don't have ground glass in them, so they don't melt when they're heated the way regular glazes do. You can paint underglazes on either greenware or bisqueware. The colors stay crisp and clear, and won't blend together like glazes. If you want to make a design on your project that has sharp, clean edges, underglazes are a good choice. Buy underglazes at ceramic supply shops. They come in jars, just like low-fire glazes. In fact, they look so much like glazes, sometimes it can be confusing! Always look carefully on the label, to see whether it says "glaze" or "underglaze."

Since underglazes can be painted on greenware, you can use them to make a special design called sgraffito (pronounced scruh-FEE-toe). Sgraffito is made by scratching a design through a layer of underglaze, to show the clay that's underneath it. Sgraffito designs work best on pieces that have not yet been bisque-fired. Here is how to put on a sgraffito design.

What You Need

Finished greenware project (hasn't been fired yet)

Newspaper

2 or 3 small, 2-ounce (56 g) jars of non-toxic, lead free underglaze, any colors

Paintbrushes

Water for rinsing brushes

Sharpened pencil

What to Do

1. Spread newspaper over your work area. Place the unfired project on the paper in front of you. (In the photos, Hunter is painting an Egyptian pyramid.) You can paint underglazes a few hours after you've finished making the project, or wait until it's completely dry.

2. Thoroughly shake the jar of underglaze before you open it. Paint two coats of underglaze on the outside of the pyramid. Let the first coat dry a few minutes before putting on the second coat. You can use more than one color if you want. It's fun to paint different parts of your project different colors (see photo 1). Be sure to rinse the paintbrush before putting it into a new color.

3. Wait for the underglaze to dry. If the clay is dry, the underglaze will dry in a few minutes. If the clay is wet, it will take a little longer. When the underglaze is dry, use a sharpened pencil to draw your sgraffito design into the underglaze (see photo 2). The pencil will scrape away some of the underglaze to show the clay underneath. If you're painting the Egyptian Pyramid Project, try drawing a brick design this way, to show how the real Egyptian pyramids were made. Or make hieroglyphic symbols, such as an eye or the sun. You could even draw Egyptians riding across the desert on camels! To make different kinds of lines, try some other tools, such as the pin tool, a toothpick, a comb, or a disposable plastic fork.

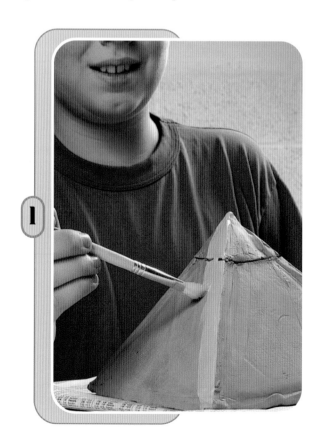

4. When you're done, let the project dry completely. Then it's ready to be bisque fired. After the bisque firing, the underglazes will be fused into the clay, like stains. If you touch them, the colors won't smear or come off.

5. To give your bisque-fired project a glossy, waterproof coating, paint a low-fire, clear transparent glaze over the underglazes. Be sure to follow all the rules for glazing, using wax resist on the bottom and on the edges of the lid, if your piece has one. Clear glazes usually look white or pink once they're painted on. After it's fired, the glaze will turn clear, and your sgraffito design will show through it.

Kilns and Firing

Potters use many different types of kilns to fire their pots. There are salt kilns, gas kilns, raku kilns, bonfire kilns, and many more. Each different type of kiln gives clay creations a different look. In the next section, you'll learn how to make a sawdust kiln from a metal garbage can.

If your school or recreation center has a kiln, it's probably an electric kiln. Pottery glazed with low-fire glazes are usually fired in an electric kiln. In an electric kiln, the pieces are stacked on removable, fireproof shelves (see photo 1). As much space in the kiln as possible is filled up with pots. For the bisque firing, pots can be stacked so that they're touching each other. A dial on the kiln controls the temperature, which must be increased gradually, until the kiln is hot enough to "cook" the clay.

In the glaze firing, pots are placed as close together as possible, but not so close that they touch. Pots that touch in a glaze firing will stick to each other forever! Also, glaze must be wiped off the bottom of a pot so it won't stick to the kiln shelf. Again, the kiln operator gradually raises the temperature, until it's hot enough for the glazes to melt.

An electric kiln has a special round hole in it called a *peephole*. The kiln operator (who wears protective glasses) can peep into this hole to see how the firing is progressing. Just inside the peephole sits a triangular-shaped piece of ceramic material, called a cone (see photo 2). The cone is specially made to melt at a certain temperature. By checking the cone through the peephole, the kiln operator knows when the kiln has reached the correct temperature.

Sawdust Kiln

The projects in this book were all fired in an electric kiln, but you might want to try this fun way to fire a project or two instead.

In ancient times, people used wood to fire their pots. You can make a sawdust kiln to give your pots a smoked, aged look. Be sure to get a grownup to help you with the firing. You'll need an open space, away from trees, bushes, and buildings. Sawdust kilns make a lot of smoke, so make sure the neighbors don't mind! It's best to put bisque-fired pieces in a sawdust kiln. You can try it with greenware pieces that are completely dry, but they run a greater risk of cracking during the firing. Underglazes work well for making designs on your pot before you put it in the sawdust kiln.

Pottery that has been fired this way will have a dark, smoky look. They make interesting pieces to put in your room and admire. Sawdust-fired pottery isn't completely waterproof, so don't use your pot to eat or drink from.

What You Need

An adult to help you
Metal garbage can
Hammer
Large nail
Garbage bag full of dry sawdust
Newspaper
Matches
Leather work gloves
Bucket of water or garden hose

What to Do

1. Use the hammer and nail to punch holes all around the garbage can. Make them 6 to 8 inches (15.2 to 20.3 cm) apart, until the can's sides and lid are covered with holes.

2. Place the garbage can on a flat surface, in an open area, away from anything that could catch fire.

3. Line the bottom of the can with 3 to 4 inches (7.6 to 10.2 cm) of sawdust (see photo 1). You can get sawdust at lumberyards or woodworking shops. Many horseback riding stables use sawdust for bedding, so you can try there, too.

8. After all the sawdust has burned, wait 24 hours, until it's completely cooled, then pull out your pots. They'll be a dark, smoky color.

9. If you want them to look shinier, use a rag to rub cooking oil onto the surface. Some potters use acrylic floor wax to give their sawdust-fired pots a shine. Tung oil, which you can buy at a hardware store, also gives your pots a nice finish. Remember that sawdust-fired pots are decorative only! Never eat or drink from them.

4. Place some of your clay pieces in the sawdust, so that they're 2 to 3 inches (5.1 to 7.6 cm) apart from each other and from the sides of the garbage can. Cover them with sawdust. The insides and outsides of the pieces should be completely covered.

5. Tightly twist a couple sheets of newspaper, and place them on top of the sawdust. Keep layering sawdust, then your clay pieces, then a couple of twists of newspaper, until you're 4 to 6 inches (10.2 to 15.2 cm) from the top of the can (see photo 2).

6. Completely cover the top layer of sawdust with twists of newspaper laid side by side.

7. To be safe, make sure you have a bucket of water or a garden hose handy. Light the newspaper with matches. When the newspaper is burning well, get an adult who's wearing leather work gloves to put on the lid. The fire should smolder for several hours. If it goes out before all the sawdust burns, add some more twists of newspaper, and light it again.

Red Hot Raku

Japanese tea bowls used in the tea ceremony are fired in a special way called raku. The word raku means "happiness and comfort." In a raku firing, the tea bowls are pulled out of a wood-burning kiln with metal tongs while they're still red hot. (Potters have to be very careful not to get burned, or they won't be very happy or comfortable!) The bowls are then placed in leaves and grasses to smolder and cool. Any kind of clay creation fired in the raku method have beautiful swirls of smoky colors.

Photo by Anna Vogler

Gallery

Brianna Dolan (age 13), *African Mask*, 2000. Earthenware; 3 x 8 x 12 in. (7.6 x 20.3 x 30.5 cm). Photo by Mark Seeley

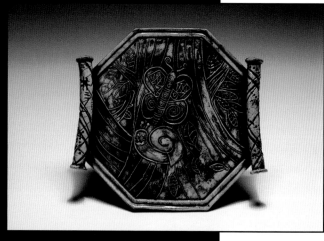

Michael Fields (age 8), *Mother Nature's Snack Tray*, 2001. Stoneware press-molded slab; underglaze wiped off highlights; fired to cone 5 in an electric kiln; 7 in. (17.8 cm) diameter. Photo by Marko Fields

Jarrity Marsh (age 10), *Under the Sea*, 2001. Stoneware slab-built box; under-glaze and sgraffito; 7 x 4 ½ x 4 ½ in. (17.8 x 11.4 x 11.4 cm). Photo by Marko Fields

Leah Lau, *Ducky*, 1999. 8 x 5 x
5 in. (20.3 x 12.7 x 12.7 cm).
Photo by Paul Kodama

Abigail Fields (age 5), *Abby's Party
Beads*, 2001. Stoneware and pony
beads carved from extruded coils;
underglaze wiped off highlights
and fired to cone 06; $^1/_2$ to 1 in.
(1.3 to 2.5 cm) diameters.
Photo by Marko Fields

Alena Lali, *Beach
Girl*, 2001. 7 x 11 x
7 in. (17.8 x 27.9 x
17.8 cm). Photo by
Paul Kodama

Walton Arts Center: Group Mural, *Waterfront*, 2001. Mosaic 2D and 3D clay slips; underglaze; clear glaze; 21 x 44 x ¹/₂ in. (53.3 x 116.8 x 1.3 cm). Photo by Sarah Hutchcroft

Walton Arts Center: Group Mural, *Wally World*, 2001. Mosaic 2D and 3D clay slips; underglaze; clear glaze; 21 x 46 x ¹/₂ in. (53.3 x 66 x 1.3 cm). Photo by Sarah Hutchcroft

Rachel Warnock (age 13), *Candleholder*, 2001. Earthenware; 8 ¹/₂ x 5 1/2 x 6 in. (21.6 x 14 x 15.2 cm)

Max Termuehlen (age 6), *Birdhouse*, 2001. Earthenware; edging tools used on roof for stamping and carving; 7 $\frac{1}{2}$ x 6 x 4 $\frac{1}{2}$ in. (19.1 x 15.2 x 11.4 cm). Photo by Mark Seeley

Dannielle Dolan (age 11), *Winter Angel*, 2000. Earthenware; 8 $\frac{1}{4}$ x 4 x 4 in. (21 x 10.2 x 10.2 cm). Photo by Mark Seeley

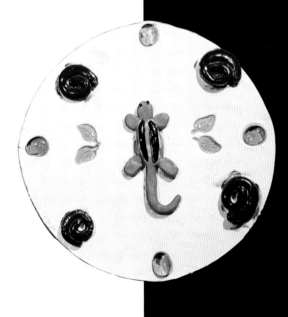

Dannielle Dolan (age 11), *Lizard Stone*, 1999. Earthenware; $\frac{3}{4}$ x 9 $\frac{1}{4}$ x 9 $\frac{1}{4}$ in. (1.9 x 23.5 x 23.5 cm). Photo by Mark Seeley

Hilary Amanda Barnett (age 9), *Decorative bowl*, 2001. Earthenware; glaze; 5 x 8 in. (12.7 x 20.3 cm). Photo by Mark Seeley

Brianna Dolan (age 13), *Rainbow Sunflower*, 2001. Earthenware; $1^1/_2$ x $11^1/_2$ x $11^1/_2$ in. (3.8 x 29.2 x 29.2 cm). Photo by Mark Seeley

Kathy Mesimer, *The Book of Life*, 1999. Earthenware; low-fire glaze; underglaze; 13 x 7 x 5 in. (33 x 17.8 x 12.7 cm).

Rachel Warnock (age 13), *Cross*, 2001. Earthenware; cutting, slipping and scoring techniques; 9 $\frac{1}{2}$ x 7 $\frac{1}{4}$ x 1 $\frac{1}{4}$ in. (24.1 x 18.4 x 3.2 cm)

Rachel Warnock (age 13), *Old Man*, 1999. Earthenware; sculpting; 5 $\frac{1}{4}$ x 3 $\frac{1}{4}$ x 5 in. (13.3 x 8.3 x 12.7 cm)

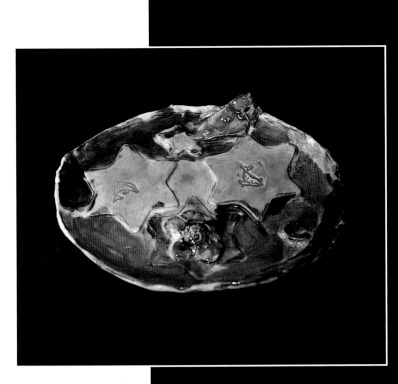

Cheryl Demeyer (age 6), *Plate*, 2001. Low-fire white clay; low-fire glaze; clear glaze. Photo by Michael Demeyer

Brooks Taylor
Johnson, *Long Tongue
Frog*, 2001. Photo by
Evan Bracken

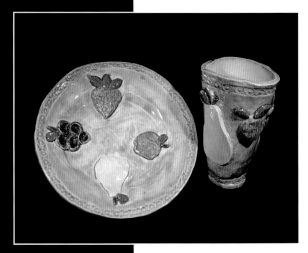

Kezra Cornell (age
12), *Fruit Plate
and Vase*, 2001.
Earthenware;
handsculpted fruit
on slab plate, 9 x 1
in. (22.9 x 2.5
cm); and slab
vase, 6 1/2 x 4 x
3.5 in. (16.5 x 10.2
x 8.9 cm). Photo
by Mark Seely

Taylor Phillips, *Hippogriff*,
2001. Photo by Evan Bracken

Carson Ellis (age 10), *Duck*, 2000. Photo by Evan Bracken

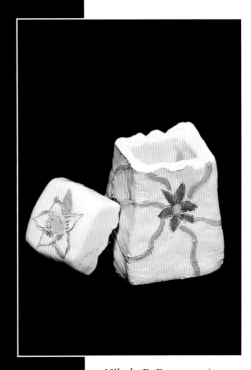

Nikole E. Freeman (age 10), *Flower Keepsake Box*, 2001. Glazed earthenware; 5 x 3 ¹/₂ x 3 ¹/₂ in. (12.7 x 8.9 x 8.9 cm). Photo by Mark Seeley

Gina Lia Ledusa (age 13), *Indian Drum*, 2000. Slab-built drum with surface carvings; wooden beads; colored feathers; 6 x 6 ¹/₂ x 6 ¹/₂ in. (15.2 x 16.5 x 16.5 cm). Photo by Mark Seeley

Jessica Demeyer
(age 8), *Bowl*, 2001.
Low-fire white clay;
low-fire glaze; clear
glaze. Photo by
Michael Demeyer

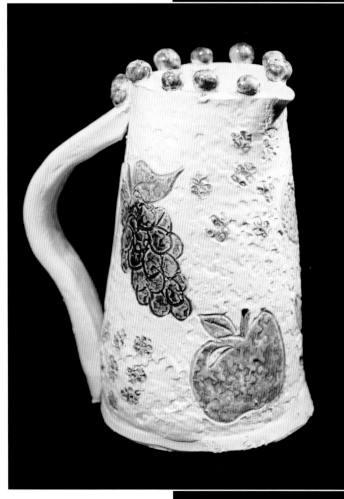

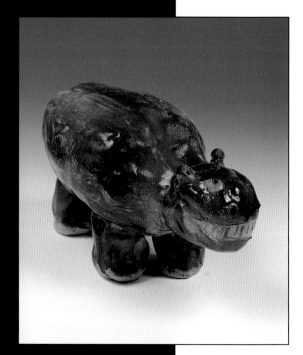

Carson Ellis (age 10),
Smiling Hippo, 2000.
Photo by Evan Bracken

Sarah Miller (age 12), *Pitcher
of Fruit*, 2001. Earthenware;
sculpted beads; 9 x 6 ³/₄ x 5 ¹/₂
in. (22.9 x 17.3 x 14 cm). Photo
by Mark Seeley

Gina Lia Ledusa (age 13), *Sunny's Lighthouse*, 2000. Earthenware formed slab with carving and small stairs cut from a slab attached to surface; 7 x 4 x 4 in. (17.8 x 10.2 x 10.2 cm). Photo by Mark Seeley

Max Termuehlen (age 6), *Compote*, 2001. Earthenware; slab bowl with decoration; 5 x 6 x 6 in. (12.7 x 15.2 x 15.2 cm). Photo by Mark Seeley

Jamiee Leigh Maeda, *Colorful Cat*, 2001. Photo by Paul Kodama

Brittany Jencks (age 11), *Bunny*, 2001. Photo by Evan Bracken

Nathaniel Humphreys (age 7), *Stirrup Vessels*, 2001. Photo by Evan Bracken

Jessica Nelson, *Shop 'Til You Drop*, 2000. Clay

Samuel Humphreys (age 13), *Snapping Turtle*, 1999. Earthenware; 12 x 11 x 4 in. (30.5 x 27.9 x 10.2 cm).

Crystal McLin, *Head Full of Thoughts*, 1998. Earthenware; low-fire glazes; 5 x 4 x 4 in. (12.7 x 10.2 x 10.2 cm)

Joshua Sinclair (age 10), *Untitled*, 2000. Earthenware; black glaze; 12 x 5 x 5 in. (30.5 x 12.7 x 12.7 cm)

Nikole E. Freeman (age 10), *Easter Floral Crucifix*, 2001. Glazed earthenware; 10 x 8 x ¼ in. (25.4 x 20.3 x .6 cm). Photo by Mark Seeley

Amanda Rose Leslie (age 7), *Loopy Woman*, 2000. Glazed earthenware; 10 x 5 x 2 in. (25.4 x 12.7 x 5 cm). Photo by Mark Seeley

Max Termuehlen (age 6), *Race Car Picture*, 2001. Earthenware; 9 x 9 x ½ in. (22.9 x 22.9 x 1.3 cm). Photo by Mark Seeley

Jessica Demeyer (age 8), *Cup*, 2001. Low-fire white clay; low-fire glaze; clear glaze. Photo by Michael Demeyer

Cheryl Demeyer (age 6), *Cup*, 2001. Low-fire white clay; low-fire glaze; clear glaze. Photo by Michael Demeyer

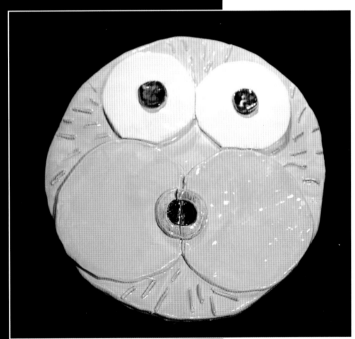

Nikole E. Freeman (age 10), *Puffer Fish*, 2001. Glazed earthenware; 10 x 10 x $^{1}/_{2}$ in. (25.4 x 25.4 x 1.3 cm). Photo by Mark Seeley

Madeline Rees (age 5), *Maddie's Creation*, 2001. Stoneware press-molded slab; underglaze wiped off highlights and fired to cone 5 (electric kiln); 7 in. (17.8 cm) diameter. Photo by Marko Fields

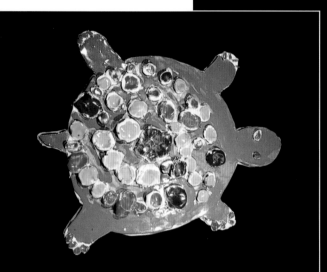

Andrew James Foy (age 5), *Flying Gamra*, 2001. Earthenware; hand-sculpted decorations; 14½ x 10 x 1½ in. (36.8 x 25.4 x 3.8 cm). Photo by Mark Seeley

Justin Tomomatsu, *Hot Rock*, 1999. Photo by Paul Kodama

Max Termuehlen (age 6), *Dog Pencil Holder*, 2001. Earthenware; 5 x 11 x 2 ½ in. (12.7 x 27.9 x 6.4 cm). Photo by Mark Seeley

Nikole E. Freeman (age 10), *Lighthouse*, 2000. Glazed earthenware; 7 x 4 x 4 in. (17.8 x 10.2 x 10.2 cm). Photo by Mark Seeley

James Y. L. M. Maeda, *Fat Unicorn Fish*, 2001. Photo by Paul Kodama

Glossary

Bisque or bisqueware—A clay piece that has been fired at a low temperature to prepare it for glazing

Bisque firing—The first firing in a kiln, at a low temperature; designed to harden and completely remove all moisture from a clay piece so that glazes can be safely applied

Bone dry—The stage at which an unfired clay piece is completely dry. Bone dry clay looks and feels chalky

Ceramics—Any clay piece fired in a kiln to make it hard and durable; from the Greek word *keramos*, meaning burned earth

Clear overglaze—A glossy, transparent glaze, usually applied over an underglaze

Coil—A ropelike piece of clay; used in handbuilding

Cone—A small, cone-shaped piece of ceramic material formulated to melt at a specific temperature. Kiln operators determine the temperature inside a kiln by observing the cones placed there.

Decorative—A ceramic piece designed to be enjoyed as an art object, such as a sculpture

Firing—The process of heating pottery inside a kiln

Foot—A supporting rim of clay at the base of a pot

Functional—A ceramic piece that has a useful purpose, such as a cup or a bowl

Glaze—A glasslike coating that melts and bonds with clay when heated to a high temperature

Glaze firing—The second firing that heats glazed clay pieces to a high temperature, causing the glazes to melt and form a glassy coating

Glaze, low-fire—Low-fire glazes are formulated to melt at relatively low temperatures, between cone 06 and 04.

Glaze high-fire—High-fire glazes are formulated to melt at high temperatures, usually between cone 5 and 10.

Greenware—Any unfired clay project

Kiln—A special oven in which clay objects are heated, or fired

Peephole—A small opening in the side of a kiln through which the kiln operator can observe the cones during firing. Special glasses should be worn to protect the eyes when observing a firing.

Pinch—A handbuilding method of squeezing clay between the fingers to shape it

Pottery—Art or craft objects made from clay

Scoring—Scratching the surface of the clay where another piece will be joined to it

Sealing—Thoroughly smoothing the seam where the two clay pieces join

Sgraffito—A decoration technique made by scratching a design through an underglaze, to reveal the clay underneath

Silica—A powdery, glasslike material that is found in all clays and glazes

Slab—A flat, even piece of clay, used for handbuilding

Slurry—A mixture of clay and water, used to hold clay pieces together

Stiffen—To dry clay very slightly so it is still moist, but somewhat harder

Tired—Clay that has lost some of its moisture and plasticity through overwork

Underglaze—A type of stain, which can be applied to greenware or bisqueware; usually used with a clear overglaze. Greenware pieces with underglaze designs must be bisque fired before adding a clear overglaze.

Wax resist—A liquid wax that repels glaze. Wax resist is added to the bottom or lid of a bisqued piece before applying glaze.

Wedging—To knead clay as a means of improving its consistency

A Note About Suppliers

Usually, the supplies you need for making the projects in Lark books can be found at your local craft supply store, discount mart, home improvement center, or retail shop relevant to the topic of the book. Occasionally, however, you may need to buy materials or tools from specialty suppliers. In order to provide you with the most up-to-date information, we have created a list of suppliers on our Web site, which we update on a regular basis. Visit us at www.larkbooks.com, click on "Craft Supply Sources," and then click on the relevant topic. You will find numerous companies listed with their web address and/or mailing address and phone number.

About the Author

Mary Ellis lives with her artist husband and two daughters near Asheville, North Carolina, in a house she and her husband designed and built themselves. She has a bachelor's degree in Art History, a teaching degree in Art Education, plus a lifelong interest in ceramics. Combining these interests, she has spent the last six years teaching children's pottery at the Odyssey Center for the Ceramic Arts.

"I discovered pottery at the age of four or five in a neighbor's basement studio. Given a lump of clay, I made a rather lumpy ashtray. To my wonderment, this object was fired in a kiln and became a solid and (to my eyes) beautiful ashtray, coated in a lovely chartreuse glaze I had chosen myself. My feeling of accomplishment became even greater when at my parents' next cocktail party for the English Department professors, all the professors wanted to use my ashtray!

I have never forgotten that feeling of importance, nor my wonderment at the seemingly magical process of turning a lump of clay into a beautiful, useful object. It's been my joy and pleasure to share the wonder of clay with the many talented and important children who have taken classes at the Odyssey Center."

Acknowledgments

Thanks go to Mark Burleson, director of the Odyssey Center for the Ceramic Arts, who first suggested I write this book;
Gail and Brian McCarthy, founders of the Odyssey Center, for their continual support of the kids' ceramic programs there;
my editor, Suzanne J. E. Tourtillot, for her skillfull editing and cheerful good nature; my art director, Tom Metcalf, for his keen eye
and playful enthusiasm; my husband, Starcen, and daughters, Emily and Carson, for their patience and support;
my parents, Lillian and Frank Moore (one a potter, the other a writer), for all their help and suggestions;
Jackie Allen, director of the children's programs at the North Carolina Pottery Center, for sending me all those slides;
Rain Newcombe, assistant editor; Orrin Lundgen, illustrator; and Evan Bracken, photographer; and special thanks to all the
wonderful, creative kids who contributed their time, ideas, and beautiful pottery in the making of this book: Sarah, Otis, Portia,
Brandy, Carson, Alice, Hunter, Amanda, Taylor, Greggory, Lily, Miles, Ross, April, Henry, Alexandara, Emily, Trevor, Nathan,
Rebecca, Abigail, Colin, Jessica, Hannah, Sam, Nathaniel, Sierra, Julia, Steven, Jaclyn, Jordan, Laura, Galen, Brooks, Graham,
Patrick, Nik, and Peyton (whew!).

Index